IF ONLY

ELIZABETH COLLEY

IF ONLY

A True Story of Unconditional Love

ELIZABETH COLLEY

This book is dedicated to my husband Mick and children
Karen, Julie, Mark and Simon

To everything there is a season,
And a time to every purpose under the heaven:
A time to be born, and a time to die;
A time to plant, and a time to pluck up that which is planted
A time to kill, and a time to heal;
A time to break down, and a time to build up;
A time to weep, and a time to laugh;
A time to mourn, and a time to dance;
A time to cast away stones, and a time to gather stones together;
A time to embrace, and a time to refrain from embracing;
A time to get, and a time to lose;
A time to keep, and a time to cast away;
A time to rend, and a time to sew;
A time to keep silence, and a time to speak
A time to love, and a time to hate;
A time of war, and a time of peace.

KJV Ecclesiastes 3:1-8

Contents

Acknowledgments

This book is dedicated to my husband Mick whose support and encouragement gave me the confidence to put my innermost feelings into words. Not forgetting my children Karen, Julie, Mark and Simon. Without them my book would not have been possible.

Every reasonable care has been taken to avoid any copyright infringements, but should any arise then I will look to correct it in subsequent editions.

Trust in the Lord with all thine heart, and lean not unto thine own understanding, in all thy ways acknowledge him and he will direct thy paths"

KJV Proverbs 3:5

Little did I realise what an impact those few words would have on my life in the future and the strength that I would need to have, as I poured out my heart to God in prayer.

This is my story.

Chapter I - The Big Day

Our birth is but a sleep and a forgetting:
The Soul that rises with us, our life's Star,
Hath had elsewhere its setting,
And cometh from afar:
Not in entire forgetfulness,
And not in utter nakedness,
But trailing clouds of glory do we come
From God who is our home

William Wordsworth

The year was 1965. My husband Ken, two daughters Karen and Julie and I were living in Higher Crumpsall, Manchester, England. It had been a long night as I awaited the birth of my third child. I timed my contractions. They were quite irregular and had started shortly before retiring to bed. They continued spasmodically throughout the night and I tried to snatch what little sleep I could aware that I was likely to get very little in the hours that lay ahead.

Morning came as a happy release and I performed my usual chores and routine: preparing breakfast, dressing the children and seeing my eldest child off to school.

By this time my midwife had been informed, and she arrived shortly after to assist me with the impending birth. I had decided to have the baby at home, following two less than desirable hospital births.

I felt very apprehensive, but these fears were soon put to rest by my wonderful midwife who never left my side.

Unlike my previous two babies the experience was much more intimate and my fear soon left me. My labor had been slow but at 12:45pm on the 25th of May 1965 following a severe thunderstorm, my darling son Paul made his entrance into the world. As a child, I witnessed a cow being struck dead by lightning and being transported off in a lorry. Witnessing that scene left me very afraid of thunderstorms so whether that played a part in speeding up my contractions, I have no idea, but I do remember, following one clap of severe thunder and lightning everything moved at a very fast rate!

This is the house in Manchester where Paul was born.
The top left window is the room where he came into the world

Paul was all I could have wished for: weighing in at 7lbs 8 ounces he was perfectly formed and a beautiful baby. I felt so proud and we bonded immediately.

My two previous daughters were only breastfed for a short while due to severe complications. I had decided in advance that I would bottle feed Paul rather than suffer the pain of previous attempts. I remember vividly the pain I endured as I struggled with breast feeding my first daughter. My breasts were bandaged up and every few hours a nurse would sit either side of me as they kneaded the lumps of milk from my swollen breasts; it was incredibly painful.

I was determined to make the effort once again when my second daughter was born but the problem re-occurred and I remember sitting and crying alone in my home with no one to turn to.

IF ONLY I had been given the support mothers are given these days maybe I would have succeeded, but I struggled alone with little help from anyone.

Did I feel a failure? At first I did. I wanted to do everything so right and be the perfect mother but life isn't always perfect as I would come to learn in the years that lay ahead.

I felt so happy and loved my role as a mother. Paul was a very easy baby and settled into a routine very quickly. He brought me great joy and I remember him having lovely thick eyelashes that most women would die for and eyes so blue they would melt the hardest heart and brighten the dullest day.

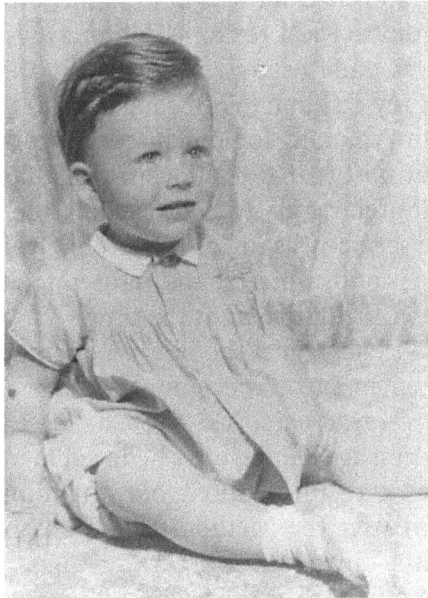

Photograph of Paul as a baby

I relished being a Mum; my children were everything to me. Many of those around me were working mothers, but all

I had ever wanted was to be a mother and to be there for my family day and night.

I had determined from a very young age that I was going to marry, live in a rose covered cottage, and have two boys and two girls, the perfect family. Maybe I was a dreamer but we all need to dream at times.

The days and months passed with my family life being the focus of my existence.

Prior to my marriage I had accepted my husband's suggestion that I meet with the Catholic Father (priest) to receive counsel and instruction on his faith, and I was happy to agree to this to understand what was required of me before I took my marriage vows.

I would meet with him each Friday after work and listen as he shared with me the Catholic faith and instructed me as to the requirements necessary for me to convert to my husband's faith.

The priest was a pleasant, kind and humble man and made me feel very comfortable but I felt quite empty during my weeks with him and did not feel ready to commit myself to another faith when I was quite happy with my own. The requirement though was for my children to be brought up as Catholics and I agreed to this not thinking too much about it at the time.

I did my utmost to live a good Christian life and attended the Catholic Church regularly. Did I get anything from it? I'm afraid not. The service was in Latin and I felt isolated and very alone. My husband lost interest and refused to attend and this made it doubly difficult for me at the time.

But looking back I feel the way was being paved for me for the future when I would eventually find what I had been searching for over the years.

From a young age I had always believed in my Savior Jesus Christ and was a regular churchgoer attending the Church of England and later the Methodist Church and thoroughly enjoying my time during those years.

I had kept a picture of the Savior by my bed and said my prayers each night. I felt so proud when I received a book for good attendance at Church and a fully stamped card, one for each week I had attended during the year.

In those days the Sabbath was strictly kept compared

to today and shops would close. Families would go for their weekly stroll in the countryside. We walked for miles and, in fact, my father and mother continued to do so every day until it became impossible due to their age and health.

When my children came along I too walked for miles: Paul in his pram, Julie on a seat on top and big sister Karen walking beside me. What lovely days they were and what wonderful intimate moments were spent together as we strolled in the park at Higher Crumpsall in Manchester and walked to the nearest town at Cheetham Hill.

I also remember as a child we had an anniversary each Easter at our local Church. Our parents attended to watch their children sing, recite and speak, and I would watch them to see if they were enjoying the presentation. They did and would beam with pride as I sang and spoke and endeavored to give my best.

My parents were certainly not well off but each year I had a new dress and Easter bonnet for the occasion and I remember feeling very pretty and special as I stood before them and sang my heart out.

I must add that this was the only time they attended Church but that was not unusual in those days. The children were sent off to Church and Mum would prepare the roast dinner which was something I looked forward to each Sunday.

These memories I thought of as I relaxed with my third child, and life seemed more tranquil and organised than with my first two. Does that sound familiar to you, Mums?

Paul soon settled through the night. What a blessing it was to retire to my bed, sleep undisturbed and to be able to refresh my body and soul for a new day.

Then came the teething time and many nights were broken by the pain of my little son crying for relief. I would slip downstairs and make a bottle for him and soothe him until he fell asleep. I felt so tired and weary and so relieved when one night I was left undisturbed when Paul slept throughout. My husband was on night duty at the time.

Looking back I thank my son for that wonderful blessing.

I awoke to find the house had been burgled. What a scene awaited me! A window had been broken to enable access for the intruder, possessions strewn over the floor from ransacked drawers, the electricity meter broken into and money extracted. With all that occurred that night I must have been completely worn out not to have been disturbed.

Anyone who has experienced a burglary will understand what a traumatic experience it was for me to find that someone had been into our home, and committed such a crime while the children and I slept in our beds. The police informed me I was a very lucky woman not to have disturbed the burglars. He said that they would not have hesitated in attacking me with the instrument they had used to break the lock on the electric meter which was our heavy handmade poker.

Following the break- in I found it hard to relax. I was continually searching in the cupboards and wardrobe and looking under the bed ready to pounce on any intruder. I had completely lost my confidence. Of course I never allowed my fear to be shown around my children, but I was severely shaken and I wondered whether I was passing the perpetrator in the street when I was out walking. Who could have committed this awful crime? Was it someone who knew me?

After the burglary Ken, my husband, suggested we buy a dog to give me more protection and help me feel a little more secure. Nicky, a Labrador puppy joined the family and we tried to move on with our life.

Locks were put on two of the downstairs doors and windows for added security, but it did not deter the intruder from breaking into our home six weeks later.

Thankfully my children and I slept throughout the night undisturbed once again but I had to face the same scene when I entered the sitting room.

The locks on one of the doors and window had been broken and chaos reigned once again.

And where was Nicky? Quietly sitting amongst it all seemingly oblivious to what had taken place. He never made a sound and being a puppy not a trained guard dog had ignored the fact that this was a stranger or strangers who had entered our home.

Once again I had to go through this very traumatic

experience plus the realisation that whoever had done this obviously knew when my husband was working nights as he had been on duty on both occasions as he was a postman and at the time working nights in the sorting office.

Why am I sharing this with you? Looking back Paul saved me from serious injury or even death by sleeping during both those burglaries.

Would I be able to save him in the coming years? Time would tell.

The police had made this very clear to me, and repeated once again how fortunate we had been to sleep throughout each burglary.

My mother-in law suggested that Ken's younger brother Philip, a teenager, stay overnight to help me cope and regain my confidence when my husband was on a night shift. I was so relieved at this solution and felt more secure knowing someone would be there for security and help me regain confidence.

Sadly this was to be short-lived. Philip at this time did an early morning paper round and would leave the house before I arose. Then, I discovered money was going missing and soon it dawned on me that he might be stealing from us.

I was seriously hoping my fears were unfounded. I had a good relationship with him but I felt it would put my mind at rest if I planted some money and waited to see whether my suspicions were unfounded. I carried on with my usual routine and hoped Philip would not suspect what I had done. I allowed a few days to pass and carried on as though I was not aware that money had gone missing. Sadly my suspicions were proved correct when on checking the drawer I had placed the money in, I found some of it had been taken. I felt completely let down and so disappointed in Philip as he had been aware of the trauma I had been through and was now adding to it.

It was such a shock to know that he would put us through this after we had been burgled twice, when he was supposedly there to comfort and protect us!

Ken was very upset and decided to confront his brother, who very sheepishly confessed he had been taking money for quite a while. Although saddened and disappointed that he could steal from us after our ordeal, I decided to forgive him. He was young and foolish and I am so glad I found it in my heart to do so as I felt great love for him, and life returned to normal very quickly. He returned all the money he had stolen and felt great remorse for what he had done. A few years later he sadly died from a brain tumour after much suffering.

Thankfully we were not burgled again, but within a short space of time, our dog Nicky became very ill. He began to be very aggressive, snapping at me and frothing at the mouth, and running around in circles.I was very scared and unsure what to do but I knew I had to do something, as I felt for the safety of my children.

I called a vet out who took one look at Nicky, and without an ounce of compassion, said the dog would have to be put to sleep. The vet then declared that he needed a pair of stockings to tie Nicky's legs together while he administered the injection.

It was such a shock and I fought back the tears as Nicky took his last breath.

The vet then informed me we would need to dispose of the body ourselves and I was left with Nicky lying on the floor in an outhouse with his legs still tied together and me trying to compose myself and come to terms with what had happened.

My confidence was at an all-time low and I lived in constant fear of someone entering the house and I would be confronted again with chaos. I carried the poker around with me, and I have never fully recovered from the burglaries. To this day I cannot sleep if alone in the house without a light on.

My life in Manchester had been very difficult at times. As a child I had lived in Cornwall and had never ventured further afield than to a holiday in Great Yarmouth, which, strangely enough, would be my future home and where I had been born many years before.

Looking back to my move from Cornwall to Manchester, I remember feeling as though my heart would break as I began my new life many miles from home and how responsible I felt as we left behind those we loved, parents, brothers and friends, for a new life with my husband and daughter.

I must admit to feelings of apprehension and some

concern as to what I had let myself in for.

At that time we had no home of our own as my husband was unemployed having left the Royal Navy following his service as a steward.

My in-laws had kindly agreed to let us stay with them until we could buy our own home. First, however, my husband had to find employment and save enough money for the deposit. Very little deposit was required in those days but it took longer than we had anticipated, and we lived with Ken's parents for nearly two years. We moved into our first home just two weeks before our second child, Julie, was born.

I remember the chaos and mess with unpacked crates when I gave birth to Julie, but I was young enough to cope with it and adjusted to the situation very quickly.

My in-laws lived a short distance from us but I had to quickly adjust to being independent. Grandparents did not give the same level of support to family as they do now, and I felt very homesick and lonely at times but threw my life into being a good mother.

I did however have a good relationship with my mother-in-law and had great love for her. This relationship would remain steadfast until her death and I will always remember her with fondness.

I do recall on separate occasions having mumps and chickenpox and wanting so much to take to my bed, but had no choice but to carry on with my every day routine. By then, Ken had found employment and no other help was forthcoming.

My daughter Julie and I both went down at the same time with chickenpox. She was still a baby under two years old and very sick, indeed. I was pregnant with my son, Paul, and it was a very difficult time trying to run the home and care for everyone.

My children were my life. I cannot express the joy I felt as a mother. I had so little in the way of material things and it was difficult seeing my children's friends blessed with possessions that I could never afford for mine. I tried to make up the gap by spending long hours knitting pretty coats for them and buying assorted hair ribbons.

I felt the proudest mother in the world whenever we ventured out on our many walks together. Unlike many of our friends we had no car and we walked everywhere and this became our regular activity.

Manchester was not a healthy environment to live in. We had to contend with thick yellow smog constantly invading our lives and affecting our health. I remember at times it was so bad we had to wear scarves over our mouths when walking outside and it was very difficult to see too far ahead.

After much deliberation and pondering we made the decision to move back to the West Country where we had previously lived to enable us to give our children a better quality of life.

We put our house in Manchester up for sale, put what furniture we had into storage, and travelled down to Cornwall during the night in a hired van. We only took necessary items with us one of which was Paul's pram. I remember him sleeping in it as we travelled, with just a brake on to steady it. I often relive that memory and the risk we took at the time regarding his safety, and, of course, there were no car seat belts in those days.

We moved in with my parents in Tideford, Cornwall on a temporary basis while we waited for news from our estate agents that our house in Manchester had been sold and we could find a home of our own.

There was another reason why I had been so relieved to leave our Manchester house. We found to our dismay after purchasing it that the house was infested with cockroaches. They were everywhere upstairs, downstairs, in our shoes and on one occasion I found one in our bed. They were grotesque. I was horrified. They came out at night when all was dark and I remember my parents coming to stay with us and the fear of them finding out the extent of the cockroach infestation we were living in. I was very worried at how they might respond especially my mother who I am sure would have spent some sleepless nights had she been aware of them, and decided it would be best to refrain from telling them.

I remember one evening when I was busy knitting coats for the girls I caught out of the corner of my eye, a cockroach crawling from under the cushions on the settee. It freaked me out. We discovered that their nest was behind the fireplace and the only way we could get rid of them was for the whole row of terraced houses to be treated. Seemingly, the cockroaches were able to travel from house to house.

Unfortunately some of the tenants were not in a position to pay for the treatment so we had to learn to live with them.

For those who have heard of the soap opera *Coronation Street* which is shown regularly on television, this is the type of accommodation we lived in. We had no garden, only a backyard and alleyway at the rear, which was an ideal situation for would-be burglars.

I must confess I felt quite guilty knowing that our new tenants would unknowingly buy our house and be faced with the same problems as us, but common sense prevailed and I recognised that our house would never sell if this information was forthcoming. We, too, had had to face the same situation when purchasing, and this information had been withheld from us. But it didn't prevent me from having a guilt trip nevertheless.

It would take over a year before we were informed that we had a buyer and I am sure this must have put a strain on my parents with a family of five taking over their home for so long.

But they were so pleased to have us back and we settled in very well. I was very blessed to have well-behaved children who were taught to respect others and were disciplined with love.

Looking back I am thankful for the good principles my parents taught me: to contribute, to do my share in running the home, to be respectful and never answer back. I learned to cook and clean, pay my way, respect my home and be obedient to my parents.

But I also have vivid memories of violence in the home and seeing my mother very bruised at times and praying in my bed at night that Daddy would not kill my Mummy.

I was terrified.

I remember hiding under our neighbour's table one day. I could hear my mother and father having a terrible row and I knew that my mother would be on the end of more punishment. I thought I could block out the sound of raised voices and threats to my mother that convinced me he was going to kill her by cowering under the table to protect myself.

It is hard looking back, remembering the abuse that was part of my younger years, but also remember that I was very much loved. When peace reigned once again I felt a temporary reprieve until the next time. But the years of abuse would eventually take its toll and affect my schooling and my self-esteem.

My father's temper did mellow over the years although he would remain very controlling, and the abuse became a verbal rather than a physical one toward my mother.

But the positive attributes I learned from them would stand me in good stead in the years ahead.

As a mother myself, I was constantly being told how well-behaved, polite and respectful my children were. They have often reminded me that when they were young and played in a friend's house, they were taught to return home if the family was about to eat and to always be polite and say "thank you". At home they were not allowed to leave the table while others were still eating and had to ask before they could be excused. And litter was not to be dropped under any circumstances.

They were also to pick up and put away their own toys at all times. This brought back memories of our younger son, Simon, many years later. He was about four years old and when asked to put away his toys he refused. I remember getting hold of his hands in mine and making him pick them up. He put on a tantrum and was promptly put in his bedroom as punishment. All was quiet for a while and then I espied toys being thrown down from his room into the front garden! Simon that day was not a happy boy but he reluctantly faced his punishment and has grown into a fine young man.

My father was very strict and rules were put into place at home, but looking back I feel we all managed in difficult circumstances to lead a very structured life.

I feel a great sense of gratitude for the love and help my parents gave me. In spite of some bad memories as a child I knew my father loved me, and no doubt was the man he was because of his own difficult childhood.

There were many good times too, the memories of which I cherish.

I love and forgive my Dad unconditionally, and of course I adored my mother who was so caring and loving to us all.

IF ONLY I had felt able to tell them more often when they were alive and expressed my gratitude to them for all that they did for me and my family.

I am sure that within their heart they knew as we did have a very close relationship and we shared some very special times together. But I will always carry within my heart the regret I felt that my future might have taken a better path had my childhood been more stable. And events that would occur later on in my life could have been avoided.

Chapter II - A New Start

In 1969 we moved into 124 Renown Street, Keyham, in Devon. I truly enjoyed having my own home again. We had no garden only a backyard but this was all we had known when in Manchester so it wasn't a problem. I look back fondly at the many happy times I shared with the children sitting in the sun while they frolicked in the paddling pool in this very small and confined space.

The picture of our house was taken after we had left. Updating has taken place and looks very much improved. Note the little back yard. At the rear of the house is the Labour Club where I would eventually meet my future husband.

They were simple joys but nevertheless ones that remain longer than ones which involve material requirements.

Karen and Julie were allocated a place in Drake Primary, a local school and they settled in very quickly and happily. The Headmaster, Mr. Parish, was a very kind and helpful man and the school was very well run.

Financially, life was a struggle. My husband was a postman

and it was our only income, which with a mortgage and family of five to support did not go far in those days.

Fortunately a job became available as an assistant in a local children's nursery. I applied and was immediately accepted. In those days certain types of work did not require references and/or qualifications.

A picture of the children's nursery group. Paul is in the front and I am on the left at the back

I can remember going from one job to another with a short interview and immediate acceptance. Now it has gone to the other extreme and people are required to have qualifications even to be a cleaner. Common sense, which is all you need in many jobs, has gone out of the window.

Going back to my story, I was very blessed to be able to take Paul with me to work and he was a very happy little boy and soon settled in. I so enjoyed my time at the nursery with the children and have so many happy memories reading *Mr. Men* and other stories to the children, singing, dancing and generally making a fool of myself as I strode like an elephant, roared like a lion and purred as a kitten.

Sadly during this time, my marriage which had been floundering for some time, slowly disintegrated coming to a sad end in 1971.

I do not wish to apportion blame to anyone as it serves no purpose in my story which is primarily about my son Paul, but sadly, I felt I had no choice but to file for divorce as by this time we were all affected by the situation in some way or another.

We may try to hide our sorrow from our children, but for those who have experienced the trauma of divorce will fully understand, children can discern when something is not right.

One thing I have learned from my own experience is that divorce does no one any favors and is not something I would recommend to anyone if there is another way. Unfortunately, for some there is no alternative and decisions have to be made that can have lasting consequences. I could never have envisaged how stressful and traumatic the decision I had taken could be.

Remember, my childhood dream was to marry have four children and live happily ever after in my rose covered cottage. Does that sound familiar? Did I feel guilty? You bet I did.

How would divorce affect my children? **IF ONLY** I knew.

It took eighteen months for my divorce to be finalised due to appeals and legal procedures but eventually my decree absolute came through and I could finally move on with my life.

By this time my house had been repossessed on my solicitor's advice, a decision I would later regret. Unfortunately I could not pay the mortgage once Ken had left and I had little choice but to agree to her suggestion. The house was in my husband's sole name and I was advised by my solicitor that Ken had agreed that I could continue to live in the house provided I did not re-marry. Although I had no current plans to do so, I felt it was unfair to agree to such a request. I was still a young woman and did not know what the future would hold, so I reluctantly chose to give up my home.

Ken came to an agreement with the Nationwide Building Society to allow them to repossess the house for a sum of £3,500. Two weeks later the house sold for over £7,000.

I was mortified. The house could have been sold privately and the profit distributed on fair terms. That would have been a much better solution, but I learned through hindsight and maturity that we see things more clearly after the event at times.

A council flat was offered to me, with no alternative choice of a house and I felt great sadness as we left our home and the security I had felt within its walls. Could I have done things differently? I still do not know; **IF ONLY**

I had had the knowledge and wisdom maybe I could have had some help to remain in my home but it seemed an impossible dream at the time.

What effect would this have on my children? They were settled and happy in their school with good teachers and a happy environment. How would they feel at leaving their home, their school and the friends they had made and witness the breakup of their parent's marriage?

What would the future hold for them? **IF ONLY** I knew.

Why didn't anyone warn me how hard life could be?

I felt great sadness on the day we moved. I knew my three children would need to move schools and say goodbye to their friends as well as leave their comfortable house to live in a flat.

I outwardly appeared happy and confident and tried my best to put on a positive front for the children, but I was relieved when they had settled into their new home and schools.

I was determined to make the best of a difficult situation and tried to adjust to life on a council estate with others in similar circumstances as myself.

I felt completely out of my depth in my new environment. I had been brought up on a council estate in my youth and been happy with my life. We had good friends and divorce was little heard of in those days. But this was a little different. It seemed as though all the divorced people were housed in close proximity to one another. I felt very upset but still there was little I could do about it but accept the situation.

Many times in the future I would find myself in circumstances I would not have chosen to be in but could do little about. This prompted me many years later to buy a plaque I saw in a shop with one of my favorite sayings written by Reinhold Niebuhr on it. It has pride of place in our home and I often read it to remind me that there are some things in life we may not choose, but it is important to see that we all have to face challenges, but if we can overcome them we are strengthened and we learn so much in the process.

Here are those words and although short, contain such wise counsel:

God grant me the serenity to accept the things I cannot change; courage to change the things I can; and wisdom to know the difference.

Reinhold Niebuhr

By 1973 I had met and married my present husband Mick who was at the time serving in the Royal Navy.

Mick and I on our wedding day just after the ceremony at the Plymouth Registry Office

The children bonded with him very quickly and he was loving, caring and made them very happy. I was very cautious, and Mick often reminds me that he asked me to marry him twice before I found myself able to accept. I was afraid history might repeat itself and I had already felt a failure because my childhood dreams had been shattered. In time I began to feel more at ease and we spent many happy hours together as a family: walking, attending school events, visiting Mick's ship HMS Woodlark, and going to "Navy Days", swimming, enjoying picnics and generally enjoying life. Those are the happy memories that will remain with me forever.

Some Sundays when Mick was on duty we would go onboard his ship and he would make us lunch which was lovely. This became a family occasion when he was on duty. Paul loved to visit Mick's ship, a coastal hydrographic survey vessel based in Devonport, as he would get to do some fishing in the river.

Navy Days were wonderful and my husband was so proud to show us around the various warships berthed in Devonport dockyard, dressed in his naval uniform, and looking so smart. Later in the day we watched the "field gun" crews and listened to the Royal Marine band to finish off a lovely day. We had little in the way of material wealth but we were happy.

The only photograph of Mick in his uniform

A picnic in the park and Paul about to go fishing from a nearby pier

*Julie, Karen and Paul Fishing from Mick's survey
ship he was serving on - HMS Woodlark*

I remember on one occasion Mick decided to dismantle our kitchen cabinet and make a sledge with it for the children and they would spend many hours in a nearby field with their friends joyfully speeding down the snowy hills.

Sometimes the best things in life are those that are free.

On Bonfire Night, because we had very little money, we would watch from a distance other people letting their fireworks off from their gardens. We would eat our homemade toffee apples and drink hot chocolate from our flask, and our children to this day look back with fondness on those times and how happy we were.

Eventually Mick was drafted from HMS Woodlark to the Hydrographic Training School at HMS Drake Naval Barracks in Devonport. Paul was so happy when Mick also acquired a part-time evening and weekend job with a company called Williams, selling ice cream. Paul loved to travel with him and eat the wonderful ice cream with Devon clotted cream on the top. At the weekends the whole family would all help him on the round and end up eating far too much ice cream - too tempting to resist.

The extra money earned enabled us to have a wonderful holiday on the Norfolk Broads. Little did we know that one day we would live in Norfolk permanently.

*Our holiday on the Norfolk Broads with
Mick at the wheel of the boat*

*Karen and me at the wheel and
Paul and Julie swabbing the decks*

Our children at a stopover in Great Yarmouth during our Norfolk Broads holiday

Paul and me on the top of the boat enjoying the sun and the peacefulness of the broads

Following our holiday, my husband (with my full blessing) decided to leave the Royal Navy at the end of his contract term of 12 years. He wanted to be at home and be more of a family man. He had done his share of travelling away for months at a time and felt it was time to settle down to a more normal family life.

Paul, Julie and me

Mick left the Royal Navy in October 1973 having served from the age of 15. He often talks about that particular day and relates the feeling that as he walked out of the barrack gates. He felt very vulnerable as being in the forces was a secure environment with virtually everything provided, and as it was he did not have a job to go to. He remembers saying to himself as he walked out of the gates "What am I going to do now?" Fortunately the very next day he went to the local dairy and was immediately employed as a milkman.

At weekends Paul tried to arise early (usually between 4:30am - 5:00am) to help Mick on the milk round. This however was short lived due to his reluctance to get out of his warm bed at such an unearthly hour. But he did spend many happy hours playing football, fishing and swimming with Mick. There was a good bond forming between the children and Mick at this time.

Over the next few months, Mick was constantly looking for suitable employment as a hydrographic surveyor, and following on from several job applications; he was invited for interviews for work. On one occasion Paul accompanied him to Leatherhead, Surrey to meet with representatives from the Decca Survey Company which at that time was the UK's largest offshore survey company. While Mick was being interviewed Paul was entertained and generally spoiled by people who worked there and was treated to soft drinks and sweets.

He was very popular and with his beautiful blue eyes and thick eyelashes and soon had people eating out of his hand.

Mick was offered the job but decided to see if other work turned up that might be more suitable.

We had to think very carefully before making any decisions as it would entail moving and the children were settled in their schools and doing well.

On Paul's 9th birthday he went off to school as usual and we had arranged to celebrate his birthday when he arrived home. Meanwhile we erected a tent, one of his presents, in the back garden and put all his birthday food inside. As we led him out into the garden his face said it all. He was so happy and excited to see the tent he had so badly wanted. He almost tumbled into the tent so great was his excitement. Alas! The food we had so carefully prepared and set out on a sheet to surprise him was being devoured by hundreds of ants. After the initial shock Paul was able to see the funny side of the situation and took it very well. Fresh food was again prepared but this time eaten inside the house. We often laugh at the memories of that fateful day.

Paul could be so funny. He loved to hide behind the curtains and come out and entertain us. One of his special acts was impersonating Daffy Duck which he did to perfection. Sometimes he would go outside and while we were eating he would make funny pictures on the window to make us laugh. He had a great sense of humour and could be so entertaining.

On Sundays he and his sisters would attend the local Baptist Church which he seemed to enjoy especially as they played guitars and made it a fun time.

He also loved anything to do with nature, and would spend hours watching television programs that had any connection with animals since he hoped one day to be able to work with them. He also loved Superman, riding his bike, and telling jokes which he did so well.

I remember the time we all went to Butlin's Holiday Camp at Minehead, Devon and Paul decided to go swimming with his sisters. He was quite a competent swimmer and we felt happy to leave him for a short while knowing there were two lifeguards in attendance.

All was going well until he was pushed under by someone who was unaware that Paul was sinking fast, gasping for breath and struggling to get to the surface and drowning. He was thankfully rescued and resuscitated by the lifeguard who became aware of the situation and treated him promptly by the poolside.

Paul looked so pale and in complete shock and it was quite upsetting at the time for us all but it did not put him off swimming and he was back in the water the very next day. His life had been thankfully saved but for how long?

During our time at the holiday camp a competition was held for the best picture drawn or painted. Our two daughters were quite proficient at art so we were expecting one of them to do well, but to our surprise Paul won first prize with a less than average contribution. He was presented with a certificate and a mini golf set.

I am sure the judges came to the conclusion that as his sister's efforts were so good they may have been assisted. We will never know but Paul was one happy little boy.

Paul receiving his prize looking very pleased with himself

Chapter III -
The Downward Spiral

"If you find a path in life with no
obstacles it probably doesn't lead anywhere"

Frank A. Clark

On the 11th of May 1974 our fourth child Mark was born. Paul loved him so much and would sometimes come home in his lunch hour from school just to see his new baby brother and to feed him. He was very protective of Mark, so proud of him and thankfully he was not jealous of the new baby joining the family.

Paul feeding Mark

Paul seemed very settled, outwardly happy and had made a new friend called Johnny. They spent time together either at home or down the woods which were very close by. We were unaware but Paul was starting to change from the innocent little boy we knew and loved. Outwardly we saw no signs that would ring warning bells and our life seemed as normal as the average family with both good and bad days.

By this time Mick with his past experience in the Navy was successful in acquiring suitable employment as a hydrographic surveyor with an offshore survey company based in Great Yarmouth, Norfolk. This job would mean we would have to move home once again.

How could we uproot our children again and put them through more upheaval? This was a very difficult decision to make but Mick needed a career to support his family and I could see he very much wanted this job. I reluctantly agreed as we had very little alternative.

Remember, I had been born in Great Yarmouth but moved when I was eighteen months old to Devon with my parents, and now we were about to uproot back to my birthplace and leave behind my parents, other members of my family, and some very good friends of mine. They were naturally upset at the prospect of us moving so far away from them and would particularly miss the children. But we didn't really have a choice as career prospects as a hydrographic surveyor in Devon and Cornwall were virtually none existent. We had no home to go to and proceeded to look for a council exchange. After a number of setbacks, we did eventually find a 'house swap' with a family from Gorleston, close to Great Yarmouth.

Plans to join my husband who had already started work were put forward. This was a very stressful time because we had setback after setback with those we were exchanging with. The couple who had originally been interested in the exchange were now putting obstacles in the way. We even sought the advice of a local politician to see if he could be of assistance to us. He was very polite but was unable to make any progress. Sadly the house exchange finally fell through and we had to begin all over again looking for suitable accommodation.

It was a very testing time for us and we had some very difficult decisions to make in order for us to join Mick in Norfolk.

After six weeks working away, Mick returned home and suggested we try and rent a property on a temporary basis.

After ploughing through magazines and making numerous telephone calls, he eventually found a holiday chalet in Hemsby, Norfolk which meant we could all be together again as a family. Our spirits lifted.

The move would mean giving up our council flat and all future chance of a council property. But we were determined to go ahead and had faith that all would eventually be well. The important priority was that we would be together as a family. That was all that mattered. And our new area sounded so exciting, too.

During October of 1974 we moved to Hawaii Beach near Hemsby leaving my parents to put our furniture into storage for our new home when we found one.

We hired a car, packed some clothes and other essentials, including our budgie Nicky and said a very sad farewell to my parents. The look on their faces tore at my heart and I wished I could have taken them with us at that moment. As we drove off I took one last look back at them, standing forlornly by the roadside and knew it was doubly difficult for them having left Great Yarmouth themselves, and now seeing us preparing to make a new life there for ourselves in a place that held so many memories for them.

Many years later I would be reminded of their sadness when I would say goodbye to our youngest son, Simon, as he prepared to make a new life in America.

There are mixed feelings at times like these.

IF ONLY I could have seen what lay ahead and how our life would change forever by the journey we were about to embark on.

Chapter IV - Life in Hawaii

"Keep calm and carry on"
Words of a motivational poster produced by the British government in
1939

It took around twelve hours to reach our destination. We arrived tired, and somewhat apprehensive, as we had no idea what our new home looked like. The place we had hired for our temporary home was just north of Great Yarmouth and it sounded exotic to say the least. A holiday site called Hawaii with a beautiful beach within walking distance. All we needed was the sun to complete the picture.

Did I say sun? It was wet and miserable when we arrived in Norfolk and as we got the first glimpse of our new home I was speechless. What a shock. A very rundown, tired looking chalet stood before us leaving us wondering "what on earth had we let ourselves in for"!

The place was so small I could not imagine how a family of six could live in such a confined space. There were only two very small bedrooms, a tiny sitting room with a two bar electric fire, and an even smaller kitchen. Our bedroom was to be the sitting room with a pull out sofa to sleep on.

And so began our new life in Hawaii on a wet and windy October day in 1974, but looking on the positive side, I knew it would only be for a short period while we looked around for more suitable accommodation and I was determined to make the best of our time in Hemsby and look positively to the future.

The chalet at Hawaii Beach. This photograph was taken many years after we had moved out. It looks more presentable here than when we lived in it

Unfortunately Mick was required to go and work offshore almost immediately upon our arrival. This left me with the four children to care for on my own. Before he left we did managed to settle the girls into a grammar school in Great Yarmouth, but that meant walking over a mile through muddy lanes and dark mornings to the nearest bus stop.

Paul was offered a place in the village school a round walk of two and a half miles twice a day and this became a great challenge especially as it seemed to rain daily. There were no street lights and a torch was a necessity to light the way. But I had no choice.

My youngest child, Mark, was only five months old at the time and all we owned was a very small buggy hardly ideal for the inclement weather we faced each day. To add to the growing misery, one of the wheels came off during a severe thunderstorm. I had no alternative but to endeavor to push the buggy home on three wheels for over a mile. I was not a happy woman.

Little did I realise Paul was also not happy. It was not until many years later that he shared his experiences at his new school with me and how he was treated unkindly at times by others.

Paul was a naturally quiet child and kept his emotions very much to himself. To me he appeared happy and content and never complained. Although, with hindsight, I remember he did not have friends outside of school. It was not surprising given where we were living.

Our "home" was on a seasonal holiday site, and now that the tourist season was over, there were very few other people around. This, combined with the lack of transport when Mick was away, made it very difficult to strike up friendships with anyone.

One night a knock came on the door and on opening I found the police. They informed me that most of the empty chalets had been broken into and they were checking to see if we were safe and well.

On assuring them we were they proceeded to tell us we could not remain living there because it was temporary accommodation only and we would have to vacate the property as soon as possible.

My heart sank and I wondered what on earth we were going to do.

When Mick arrived home from sea I shared with him the break-ins at the other chalets and the visit from the police. We realised we would need to look for somewhere else to live quickly, and after much deliberation and discussion, together we felt our only solution was to approach Mick's employer (owner of the company) and ask for a loan so that we would have the deposit to put on a house. At that time we had no savings in the bank and were living from one pay cheque to another.

This was a very difficult task for my husband. He was a new staff member and it was understandable that his employer would be reluctant to part with money that he had no guarantee would be returned.

We made an appointment and were very nervous at the reaction we might receive.

We mustered up what courage we could as we shared our position with him and our inability to raise the money we would need to put a deposit on a house. The atmosphere was very tense as we appealed to him and I didn't feel hopeful. I remember fighting back the tears as we related to him our circumstances and the visit from the police. He appeared from the outside quite a hard man lacking in compassion. We were left to sit and wait while he walked away to think about it.

I remember sitting with my young son Mark on my lap, and wondering what we would do if we were refused us help. We had given up everything to move closer to Micks employment and to be together as a family.

Minutes seemed like hours but on his return he agreed to lend us £1,000 as a deposit for a house but insisted we repaid the loan with interest through the bank within two years. Interest rates were quite high that year but not quite as high as the previous year of 1973 where they peaked at 13%. We had little choice but to accept, but it was a very difficult decision nevertheless knowing we would have a mortgage to pay as well. At the time my husband was only on an annual wage of £2,500 with extra benefits when working offshore which was not a life changing amount. In 1974 the basic rate of income tax was 30% which compared to today, was very much higher. But for now a cloud had been lifted and there seemed to be a light at the end of a very dark tunnel.

What a relief we felt that day.

We would face many setbacks during the time ahead as we searched for a home, and spent many weeks viewing houses only to have our hopes repeatedly dashed for one reason or another.

But eventually we saw a suitable home which would fulfil our requirements, applied for a mortgage and arranged all the legal requirements needed before proceeding with our purchase. We had so much opposition and so many difficulties that it was unbelievable but eventually everything fell into place.

The three bedroom house was located in in Caister-on-Sea and priced at £10,000. This was a little more than we would have liked but we decided to make arrangements to view it. We were not disappointed. It was to me the perfect house in a perfect place and we all agreed this was the home we wanted. The building society gave us a 90% mortgage and we arranged for our furniture to arrive from Devon on the morning of the 19th of December 1974 the day set to move into our new home.

Our luck would not hold. Just two days before on the morning of 17th, Mick received a telephone call from the solicitors stating that the building society had decided not to lend us the £9,000 because we had borrowed £1,000 from another source. In their eyes the total was classed as a 100% mortgage and this was against their lending policy.

We were devastated. What could we do now? How would we ever be in a position to buy a place of our own?

After much deliberation Mick decided to go back and try to explain the position to the company secretary as his employer was away overseas on a business trip. Thankfully an agreement was set up that we would pay the £1,000 back to the company directly from wages and not through the bank thus hoping that our mortgage from the building society of £9,000 could be reinstated. Our solicitor then put the wheels into action to get our mortgage back. We were successful but a guarantee could not be given when we would be able to take possession of the house. This was another hardship but we continued to hope it would still be on the 19th December as our furniture and other belongings were due to arrive on that day. If possession of the house was delayed further we would be in a terrible mess.

The removal men had travelled overnight from Devon and arrived at 8:30am on the 19th of December and we had the uncomfortable task of explaining to them they would have to wait until 1:30pm before they could begin to unload. This was the time when the keys to the house would hopefully be handed over to us. We explained our situation to the removal men who were very understanding and felt very sorry for us. We suggested they place all of our furniture in the main living room when we were given the keys, and told them we would do everything ourselves. They were extremely grateful as they had another delivery to make that day. Fortunately for them it was not too far away, and as they had previously planned to stay overnight in a hotel before returning to Devon the next day they were not too put out and we treated them to fish and chips to compensate for the delay.

It was all very stressful but we at least had our home just six days before Christmas.

We immediately began sorting the furniture, making up beds, unpacking crockery and cutlery, hanging our clothes in the wardrobes and all the other things that need doing when moving into a new home. It was exhausting. That evening sleep came as a welcome relief.

Over the next few days we continued to sort out all our belongings and get our house "ship-shape" as Mick would say and prepare ourselves for Christmas day.

It was an extremely hectic time but, given what we as a family had been through, I thought I was in heaven.

Chapter V -
On the Move Again

"It's better to be on the move than routed to the spot, at least you are going somewhere and not stagnating"

Michael Colley

Our new house was a six year old, semi-detached house with a fairly large garden, a garage and a telephone. What more could I ask for?

This is an updated picture with a new extension to the front of the house taken after we had vacated the home

It was wonderful to be able to live close to the shops, the schools, and I could once again sleep in a comfortable bed.

But moving again meant Paul starting yet another new school, this time at Caister–on– Sea. He seemed to settle and outwardly appeared happy and content so we were not aware that he was finding it difficult to fit in and find friends.

He enjoyed rabbit hunting with Mick and I remember one evening he came home not with a rabbit but with a hedgehog and proceeded to put it on the living room carpet. Needless to say I was having none of it and promptly put the hedgehog in a box and insisted they return it from whence it came!

Mick was very adept at making Chinese arrows which Paul loved and many a child and grandchild have been entertained by his prowess at demonstrating his skill with them. The arrows are made from a straight stick with a sharpened point at one end and the other end a flight made from thin cardboard usually from a cereal box. The arrow would be launched using not a bow but a length of string. The children loved it.

They also enjoyed fishing together. I wasn't sure Mick enjoyed it that much but never let on. One day I went into the shed where they used to keep the maggots and lo and behold they had all turned into flies. I was not happy to put it mildly but Mick and the children thought it was hilarious. And so the days, weeks and months passed with Paul seemingly happy and content.

We were aware it would take time, but outwardly we could see there weren't any signs that Paul was not adjusting to his new school.

In the meantime my husband was working offshore on a regular basis - usually two weeks on and two weeks off. This wouldn't have been our choice, but it was preferable to him staying in the navy and spending much longer periods away from home. I had to be content with this and count my blessings.

With Mick away there were to be even more difficult times ahead. I struggled alone with the four children and shed many tears because of our circumstances but I did the best I could .I wouldn't have foreseen what would happen next.

During our first year in our new home little did we realise how difficult it would be to pay a mortgage plus repay the loan from Mick's employer. On top of this, there were all the other necessary bills. The income tax being 30%, the high bank and building society interest rates, and the rocketing fuel costs meant that times were tough. Unfortunately we had taken on more than we could cope with financially. We got deeper and deeper into debt and some drastic action was needed. It became necessary for me to look for work outside the home to supplement our income.

I acquired employment in a holiday camp cleaning chalets

and this meant having to put Mark into a nursery for six days a week part-time - not something I would have chosen. But had very little choice if we were to repay our debts.

Mark was a very happy little baby and settled in very quickly and was very popular with those who took care of him. I felt a sense of relief that he was in good hands for the few hours we were apart each working day.

It gave me comfort to know that the job was seasonal and I needed to take one day at a time and just do the best that I could in difficult circumstances.

Working in a holiday camp was not something I would recommend personally. Cleaning up after some holidaymakers was totally degrading and best left to the imagination. The elderly were so clean and respectable and easy to cater for. They were the ones who left the tips, others just left a mess.

Although Mark was a very good baby and soon settled into a new routine, I felt very guilty leaving him with others. I confess that during this time I became quite depressed and struggled to look after my four children, work, and all the other responsibilities while Mick was working away from home.

I knew I had to get some help with the way I was feeling and decided to see my local doctor. He was so compassionate and listened quietly as I reeled off my feelings to him of my struggles and concerns and my feelings of loneliness even though I had my lovely family to care for.

He was such a lovely man and looking back I have much to thank him for. He said he would like to introduce me to a lady who happened to be at the surgery that day and who lived around the corner from me. He thought she might be able to befriend me.

He said she was a Mormon which meant very little to me at the time.

But what did I have to lose? And so I reluctantly agreed and on being introduced to her found she was a member of The Church of Jesus Christ of Latter Day Saints, commonly known as a Mormon.

I was later reminded by my husband that missionaries from that Church had knocked on our door in Plymouth but I had made it clear I was not interested as I had never heard of the religion at the time.

Unbeknown to me Mick had hidden some literature in our shed to read quietly without my knowledge. He had felt touched by the missionary's message. Looking back I do not feel I was ready for the gospel at that time although I had always believed in God. As a child I attended Church three times on a Sunday and used to pray in my own way, although I must confess they were prayers of pleading rather than of thanks because of the constant frightening rows my parents had.

I believe the way was being paved for me in unexpected ways and that God was aware of my searching and would eventually lead me to the truth.

Chapter VI -
The Gospel in My Life

"A friendship doubles your joys and halves your sorrows"

Author Unknown

My new friend, Pauline, seemed genuinely concerned for me and very kindly invited me into her home and listened. I shared my feelings with her about the loneliness I was experiencing.

She said she was a regular Church-goer and was putting on a social event in a few days. She then invited me to come and help and hopefully enjoy some time with her friends and get to know others of her faith.

She proceeded to make me a cup of tea and explained that she did not drink tea or coffee herself as it was not part of her faith but I thought little of it at the time.

My first impressions of the Mormons were very positive. I was made to feel part of their special evening which was a Relief Society Social held annually for the "sisters" as she called them to celebrate the anniversary of the beginning of Relief Society which had been first organised back in 1842.

I became curious as to their beliefs and asked for more information as I felt good about the things she was sharing with me.

We were introduced to two missionaries, Elder Kevin Allred and Elder Jim Hallberg, who were from America and we were taught the gospel of Jesus Christ in our home. At first, Mick was reluctant to share my good news or attend Church but it was not long before he joined in and he too felt good about the things we were being taught. Later we would learn that the feelings we were experiencing were the promptings of the Holy Ghost.

We shared some wonderful times with the missionaries and a close bond was formed with them.

We were taught The Plan of Salvation and watched a lovely

film called "Man's Search for Happiness" which explained where we came from, why we are here and where we can go after this life. I have watched it many times since and it never fails to touch my spirit.

We were taught about Jesus Christ and his life here on the earth, of his death and resurrection, the apostasy that occurred after the last Apostle's death and a restoration that would come to pass in the future.

We were taught about the restoration of the gospel through the Prophet Joseph Smith who when he was in his fifteenth year was confused at the different religions at that time who were teaching different doctrines, and how he was undecided as to which Church to join.

As he was studying his Bible one day he read from James, Chapter 1: 5-6.

"If any of you lack wisdom let him ask of God, that giveth to all men liberally, and upbraideth not; and it shall be given him."

"But let him ask in faith, nothing wavering. For he that wavereth is like a wave of the sea driven with the wind and tossed."

Joseph decided he would ask God which Church he should join as he was very confused at the various religions who were teaching different doctrine. He then went to a grove of trees near his home and knelt in silent prayer. In this silent prayer he received a wonderful vision of Heavenly Father and His Son Jesus Christ. Because of that vision and the things he learned and the events that followed over the following years, we now have the restored Church of Jesus Christ on the earth today. A Church that is run as it was in Christ's day with Jesus Christ as the head directing his affairs through living Prophets and Apostles.

Assisting the full time missionaries were Stake missionaries, Len and Connie Webster, who lived nearby and some wonderful evenings were spent together discussing the gospel and getting to know one another better.

We were taught at each lesson the basic principles of the gospel and it seemed as though the missing pieces of a jigsaw were finally completed.

I had found what I had been unknowingly seeking for years.

When the missionaries challenged us to baptism I remember my husband saying, 'I've been waiting and wondering when you were going to ask'.

We felt so right about joining the Church as we had felt for some time that this is what we wanted and the spirit had confirmed our feelings that this truly was the restored Church of Jesus Christ.

The Church of Jesus Christ of Latter Day Saints Chapel in Gorleston

Len and Connie were in-laws to Pauline and we spent many wonderful times together as friends.

During this time Pauline informed me she held Primary in her home during the week for the young children whose ages ranged from three to twelve years.

These were midweek classes additional to Church on Sunday and the children were taught basic principles of the gospel suited to their ages in addition to having fun time.

She was at that time short of a teacher for the three year olds and asked me if I could temporarily teach the youngest ones while she was temporarily unavailable.

I happily accepted and as I taught and met with these wonderful children I forgot my own feelings of despair and loneliness.

Within six weeks four of our family excluding Mick was baptised. Unfortunately he was required to work offshore and had to go away just two days before the big day.

Paul just before he was baptised

It was a wonderful baptismal service followed by some light refreshments at Pauline and her husband Alan's home. Later, I was asked to give my first prayer and felt confident and happy as our evening came to a close. I thanked my Heavenly Father for the special spirit we had felt that night.

A few days later we enjoyed Christmas with the missionaries and celebrated for the first time without alcohol and it was a wonderful and happy time for us all.

My husband Mick was baptised when he returned from his work on the 19th of January 1976. My life changed and I knew that what I had been seeking for all my life I had at last found. I felt the spirit so strong and felt so happy at last.

One of the lessons taught to us was the Word of Wisdom. We were told our bodies are Temples of God and we should treat them with respect and not take into them things that might be harmful. Part of the Mormon faith was to abstain from alcohol, tobacco and other harmful or habit-forming substances.

I did not have a problem with this and knew from the experiences my mother previously shared with me, the devastating effect alcohol can have on the family when a loved one is addicted to drink.

My maternal grandmother had died at the age of 38 years old leaving behind three young children. I remember my mother sharing how hard her life was and how her mother would sell their clothes to feed her habit.

True, some would argue that a drink now and again can do no harm, but I also know an alcoholic starts off with just one drink.

I have no idea who wrote the following but I still have it in my possession and I often read it:

Alcohol the Great Remover

"Alcohol will remove stains from clothing.
It will also remove spring, summer, autumn, and winter clothing from a man, and children.
If used in sufficient quantities, Alcohol will remove furniture from homes, rugs from the floor, food from the table, lining from the stomach, vision from the eyes and judgment from the mind.
Alcohol will also remove reputations, jobs, friends, and happiness from children's hearts, sanity, freedom and a man's ability to adjust and live with his neighbour.
It even removes life itself.
As a remover of things, alcohol has few equals".

Author Unknown

They are strong words but oh so true.

I was happy to give up alcohol and knew it important to do so and to this day I have no regrets at the decision I made to abstain.

We threw ourselves into our new life in the Church and within a couple of weeks were giving a family presentation during Sunday School. The theme was based on "Love" and was very well received by the congregation.

Our girls attended "Young Women", "Paul", "Young Men" and I was busy teaching Primary and the "Young Women" and became a Visiting Teacher.

To be a visiting teacher one is assigned a sister companion and allocated several sisters to visit once a month.

Visiting Teachers give a spiritual message and generally "watch over" those who are assigned to them.

This way the females can be taken care of, emotionally, spiritually and also temporal help is given when needs arise.

The men (or "brothers" as we call them) were assigned as Home Teachers and would have the responsibility of all family members assigned to them thus lessening the "load" of the Bishop of the Ward.

Male members from the age of twelve receive the

Priesthood beginning with the Aaronic and progressing to Melchizedek when they are ready and worthy. Twelve to eighteen year olds and new male members initially receive the Aaronic Priesthood and then progress to the Melchizedek Priesthood.

As a young man Paul received the Aaronic Priesthood and I felt very proud as I watched him pass the Sacrament on a Sunday and carry out other responsibilities.

Our Bishop often commented on how smart Paul looked and how diligent he was in carrying out his duties and that we should be very proud of him and of course we were.

I remember him appealing to members of the Ward to raise funds for the Church and Paul decided to ask our friend Connie who lived close by if he could do anything for her to earn some money. She was happy to support him and gave him some silver to clean and according to Connie he made a very good job of it.

He also cleaned their car and they seemed happy and satisfied at the time, although they may have exaggerated somewhat to encourage him as he was so happy to be raising money for the Church.

He was very excited as he shared with us how much he had been paid and couldn't wait to give it to the Bishop.

On another occasion Connie had badly burned her eyes using a sun lamp and Paul decided he would spend his pocket money on a little get well gift for her.

He was a son to be proud of and the Bishop often remarked at what a polite young man he was and a great example to others.

One of the challenges facing us following our baptism and a test of our faith was the requirement to pay tithing. We had accepted this principle without a murmur but were still struggling financially, and paying off our debts but we had made the promise that we would be obedient to the commandment given in the bible in Malachi 3:10:

> "Bring ye all the tithes into the storehouse, that there may be meat in mine house, and prove me herewith, saith the Lord of hosts, if I will not open the windows of heaven, and pour you out a blessing, that there shall not be room enough to receive it."

Our very wise Bishop at that time helped and supported us and never lectured us on tithing but gave wise counsel which I will always be grateful for.

I often think it would be a wonderful world if everyone kept that commandment and paid one tenth in tithing. It would alleviate so many problems in the world that we have today, as people would be more equal, the poor would be taken care of and we would learn to love our neighbors as ourselves.

Unfortunately we don't live in a perfect world.

We concentrated on paying off our debts at first but life became such a struggle for us that we knew changes would have to be made once again.

After much prayer and fasting both Mick and I felt strongly that we needed to move home and to find a cheaper property thus enabling us to clear our debts and pay our tithing. We had such faith in the Lord and knew that He would be aware of our challenges and would be there for us so long as were faithful.

We put our home up for sale and were surprised and delighted when the first couple to view it informed us they wished to purchase it. This was a miracle in itself and we could see that prayers were beginning to be answered, but we had nowhere to move. We had not taken the time to view any prospective homes since we had not expected to sell ours so quickly. The couple made it very clear that they needed to move in very quickly and we hastily looked around for places to rent until we could decide on a house to buy but there was nothing suitably available.

We spent many hours visiting landlords and viewing various properties from houses to flats but they were either too expensive or not suitable for a family of six.

I shared my concerns with my friend Pauline the difficulty we were having and the pressure we were under to vacate our home as soon as possible. She listened quietly and then told me her husband Alan knew someone who might be able to help us. He owned property in and around Great Yarmouth and Alan very kindly offered to meet with him to see if he had anything suitable on a temporary basis for our large family.

To our relief a small house was available and we were so grateful. Or so I thought. When we went to view the property my heart sank. It was very small and dirty, and my first thought was 'I can't do this'.

The shower room was disgusting and with only two bedrooms for the six of us, and with a French student arriving soon to stay with us for two weeks, it seemed an impossible situation. To get to the second bedroom one had to walk through the first one, not an ideal situation to say the least.

To make matters worse we were told that a murder had taken place in the property and you could still see the old blood stains on the wall. Whether it was true or not I cannot say but I felt distinctly uncomfortable nevertheless.

We convinced ourselves it was only for a short time and we had little choice as the new owners of our home were putting pressure on us to move out. Reluctantly we accepted but I felt very despondent.

How were my children going to react to moving yet again and what would be their reactions when they saw the house? I need not have worried.

As always they were very understanding and accepted the situation with little murmuring but I am sure they were very sad to be leaving their lovely home. I often wonder though what truly went through their minds at that time.

Our rented accommodation

The day of moving was one which will be etched in my memory for ever. I tried hard not to show my emotions as we painfully packed up our belongings and prepared to leave the home where I had been so happy.

We had only lived there for two years so it was quite a wrench for me to walk away once again and move to a place that left little to be desired. I took one last look back as we left and I remember breaking down as we walked away, feeling such despair and guilt at putting our children through more upheaval.

But I had to convince myself that this was only temporary and we would get through this challenge as we had done before.

Just after we had moved into our rented accommodation, I vividly remember picking up the French student from the railway station and the apprehension I felt as we awaited her arrival. I wondered how she would react when we showed her where she would be staying while with us.

I kept apologising for our circumstances and remember her sweetly remarking in her French accent, 'It is so sweet' but no doubt thinking 'what have I come to?'

At a later date our daughter paid a return visit to stay with the French student's family in France to find that she lived in a wonderful large chateau with her family and they were very well off.

Following Karen's return home there was little contact with the student which was not surprising in the circumstances.

The weeks ahead were a testing time for us but I quietly said to myself that surely God was aware of our challenges, wasn't he? And he knew of our desire to serve him and keep his commandments, and having fasted and prayed surely we were doing the right thing? I could only hope this was the right decision.

IF ONLY we could see into the future sometimes.

In the meantime we started searching for another home. We spent many weeks viewing various properties and became quite despondent as nothing seemed suitable for a family of six. It was very frustrating and stressful.

Then one morning a leaflet came through the post with a description of a house for sale in Roslyn Road, Gorleston. This was very strange as we had not received property leaflets prior to this, and was the only one we would receive during the time we resided there.

Coincidence? I think not.

Armed with details of this house we made a visit to our solicitor, and spoke with the conveyancing clerk. She was very helpful and told us she was very familiar with the area. The houses were of good standing, and she felt we should "go for it". Our solicitor set up an appointment for us to see the house, and after viewing the property we both felt comfortable and it was suitable for our family, in fact we felt very good about it.

There was quite a lot of work required to improve and update but it had a welcoming feel to it. Also in our favour was the price of the property. The current market value was £10,000 but the owners finally agreed to sell at £8,250. This was great news for us as it would enable us to clear our debts and start to pay our tithing.

We agreed to purchase the property and commenced to set the wheels in motion.

I felt elated and so relieved that prayers were at last being answered. After meeting with our solicitor again an appointment was set up to meet with a building society the following Monday.

Our house in Roslyn Road taken just after we had moved in

The meeting went well and just one week later to our amazement we were called in for another meeting with the manager. We were very apprehensive but he soon put our worries to one side and with a smile told us we had the mortgage, which he said was the fastest he had ever been able to negotiate and stated that it was a miracle how quickly it had gone through.

We were shocked but nevertheless delighted.

But our joy was soon dashed again when we heard that a young couple had offered to pay cash for the house. We were devastated.

With heavy hearts we went to see the owners of the house and sadly explained our situation to them that we were unable to go ahead with the purchase immediately as it would take a couple of weeks for the money to be ready. We explained to them we could not compete with another couple who had offered to pay cash. To our amazement came another answer to our prayers and another miracle.

The couple had by this time really bonded with us and the wife responded to our concerns saying, 'My dears, my husband and I have decided that we want you to have the house and nobody else.'

I couldn't believe my ears.

What a relief and a wonderfully emotional experience. Looking back we could see that the Lord was working ahead of us and paved the way for us to have our own home, pay off our debts and pay tithing.

The owners of the house were of another faith and the husband was the organist in their Church but they were such a lovely couple and truly Christian and respected our religion for which I was grateful.

We had been blessed with wonderful neighbours at Caister who were also of another faith but again very genuine, kind and charitable. I came to realise that whatever our faith, we can love one another and live together in harmony if we truly want to.

Chapter VII –
New Beginnings

"We find the great thing in this life is not so much where we are standing but in what direction we are heading"

Oliver Wendell Holmes Sr

We moved into our new home in May and I hoped with all my heart this would be our last move. I remember the first winter in our new home.

It was bitterly cold and I was pregnant with our fifth child. Sadly I fell down the stairs and had to be taken to hospital for a termination. As I lay in bed waiting to be wheeled to theatre I struck up a conversation with a young lady who told me she was about to having an abortion as she did not want a second child. My emotions took over as here was I about to have a termination because I was losing my baby and wanting so much to keep it and she was choosing to end her pregnancy. I did not judge her for her decision as we do not always see the whole picture but it was a difficult moment for me.

I do remember lying in bed prior to being taken to hospital and it was bitterly cold. The windows in our home were so old we could not close them and ice would form on the inside.

I was happy to find that within a few months I was expecting another child. It took away the pain of losing the baby I had been expecting.

There was extensive work to be done to the house over the coming years. New windows to be installed, plus external doors, central heating and an extension at the rear of the building. This was necessary as by now our son Simon was born and there were now seven of us in the family. An extension was a much cheaper option than moving to a larger house.

To enable the work to be carried out on the house, we had

to remortgage several times but it was necessary to pay for the improvements as the house had been neglected over the years. By now, fortunately, Mick was getting a reasonable wage and we were able to make all the necessary repayments, although we had to budget and prioritise.

Having moved once again Paul felt it would be easier to leave his school at Caister-on- Sea and go to the local one which was only a five minute walk from our home and this seemed the most sensible thing to do.

He seemed happy and we felt at peace once again after so much upheaval. He made some friends and seemed more settled and confident in himself.

But the path ahead was to be a thorny one as we witnessed our son struggling at times to live up to his faith.

Looking back I do feel things might have been different **IF ONLY** Paul had had friends he could rely on but it wasn't easy. With very few young men of his age in the Church it became very difficult for him.

He did his very best but I could see it was a struggle for him to live up to the "ideal".

His new friends were pleasant but their standards were very different to the ones we were now embracing. Paul was torn between having friends outside his new faith and trying to please everyone. It was a difficult time for him. He became rebellious and told us he did not wish to continue to go to Church. This news was very upsetting for us as we were by this time very active and serving with all our heart.

We continued to encourage Paul to attend and for a time he went reluctantly but he was very unhappy and we could see it was a struggle for him as he felt so alone.

He eventually refused to attend, although we did our best to convince him that he should go and as parents tried to lead by example. By this time, however, Paul was spending much of his leisure time with his friends outside the Church and it became a struggle to keep him interested in anything spiritual.

We continued keeping our home a place of love and tried to live the gospel to the best of our ability. But it was far from easy. We talked and reasoned with Paul and let him know that we loved him and wanted the best for him.

We always tried to be a good example to Paul and explained how sad we were that he had chosen not to attend Church anymore and shared our testimony with him often. But all to no avail. His mind was made up.

There would be many other challenges that lay ahead.

We started to have problems in our home. Many people are familiar with or have heard of things that happen in the home which sometimes cannot be explained. Apparitions, feeling cold when in fact the house is warm, lights going on and off etc. Children seem to be particularly sensitive to such things.

We discovered that there was something disturbing in our home and at first we took little notice of it. On this one occasion though Mick had gone away to sea on a job and Mark who was quite young asked if he could sleep in my bed. I agreed and at bedtime I tucked him in and then went into the bathroom and started to run a bath. Suddenly Mark cried out, I rushed into the bedroom and asked what the problem was. He said 'Mum the sleeves on your dressing gown keep moving up and down'. I removed the gown from off the door and put it into the wardrobe. I spent time reassuring Mark until he was settled once more and asleep. I then returned to the bathroom. Suddenly the light-switch started switching on and off. I was very scared and ran out of the bathroom. Looking back I do not know how I got through the night.

Previous to this Mick had also had experiences in the home which were cause for concern and I knew I needed to seek help as he was away.

The following day I called one of the Priesthood holders in our Church and requested a blessing on our home.

Following the blessing, our home became peaceful again and we felt at ease once more.

Paul by this time had experienced so much upheaval in his short life that he was finding life more difficult than I could ever have envisaged. He went off to school outwardly happy at the same time each morning and returned home at the usual time so I was unaware that he was not actually going to school on a regular basis.

One day the school nurse was due to attend and I decided to be there to support Paul. When I arrived I was shocked to learn that he was not at school and had not been there for several weeks.

I was understandably upset that the staff had not taking the trouble to let me know of his absence and I voiced my feelings very strongly.

When Paul was at school he never confided in me how unhappy he was. It was years later when the truth finally surfaced but at this time he kept it to himself.

Many things came to light when he felt he was finally able to share some of his experiences.

On one occasion the school report stated that it was not possible to grade him on one particular subject as Paul had destroyed his own textbooks. Paul did not deny it because he was too scared to report to the Headmaster that they had in fact been destroyed by other boys.

He also told us how he had his head forced down a toilet and held there to humiliate him. He was picked on constantly and he lost the desire to give of best since his self-esteem was so low. Paul would not retaliate because he was small in stature and felt unable to stand up for himself. He quietly took whatever life threw at him and kept his true feelings to himself.

He was a clever boy and was top in mathematics at one time. But he lost what confidence he had had because of the way he was treated by others, but not knowing the full facts at the time, we took everything at face value.

At the time I had no reason to suspect anything or worry unnecessarily as many teenagers go through difficult stages in their lives in many different ways.

Yes, he was quiet at times and distant. He sometimes became defensive, argumentative, selfish, sullen and evasive, but again I put this down to the teenage years. I believe most parents experience times like this.

But then a pattern emerged. Items started to go missing from the home.

The first occasion was when I borrowed a lovely brooch from a friend to attend a Victorian social evening. She reminded me it was a gift from her son-in law and to take good care of it.

The evening went well and I agreed to return it promptly.

A few days later to my horror the brooch had disappeared and despite frantically searching for it, it could not be found. I shed many tears fearful of the reaction I would get when I had to confess to my friend I had mislaid her beautiful piece of jewelry knowing it meant so much to her.

I sank to my knees in prayer and pleaded with God to help me find the missing brooch and to tell him that I felt in my heart Paul had stolen it. There is no way I can explain the feelings that I had when I received an immediate answer to my prayer.

By this time I was proficient at reading my scriptures and as I knelt in earnest prayer, into my mind came the following scripture from Proverbs 3:5 "Trust in the Lord with all thine heart; and lean not unto thine own understanding. In all thy ways acknowledge him, and he shall direct thy paths".

Words cannot describe the emotion I felt as that scripture came into my mind. I felt my prayer had been answered immediately and a feeling of comfort came over me that caused me to weep.

I rose from my knees and felt a very, very strong prompting to go immediately into town and look for the brooch which had gone missing.

I spent the next two hours walking the streets and visiting the many pawn and jewelry shops to enquire as to whether anyone had sold them a brooch of the description I gave them. But it was to no avail.

By this time I was becoming very despondent and wondered what the response would be when I faced my friend with the news that I had lost her beautiful brooch.

Hadn't God directed me? I had had such a strong and intense feeling yet my searching so far had revealed nothing.

I made my way back to the bus stop and was about to turn right up into a shopping precinct when my eyes were drawn to the left of me to a gold and silver shop which I was not aware existed until that moment. My heart started to pound within me.

Why was I feeling this way?

I felt I had nothing to lose if I tried one last time to see if this was the place I was being directed to.

On entering the shop I could see a variety of items

prominently displayed in a glass cabinet before me and asked the young lady assistant whether anyone had sold a brooch to them with the description I gave her.

She was unable to help me in my enquiry but informed me that I could return later when the Manager would be back and available.

I agreed to return that afternoon and proceeded to leave.

I thanked the young lady for her help and glanced down at the display cabinet as I left where various assortments of rings and brooches were displayed. As I looked down into the cabinet, the brooch I had been looking for was right in front of my eyes and appeared to be enlarged so I would recognise it. Another coincidence? I think not.

I could only exclaim with trembling voice to the young shop assistant "That's it, that's the brooch I am looking for".

It was an overwhelming experience.

I expected to have it returned to me immediately but was advised that I needed to see the Manager on his return as she had no authority to do so without his permission.

The jewelers where I found the brooch

I left the shop feeling very relieved but also extremely upset thinking that my son had put me through such a painful time. I was still shaking but uttered a quiet "Thank you" prayer.

I immediately rang my husband at work and explained what had happened. He could hear the distress in my voice and assured me he would leave work immediately and meet up with me to give me support.

On his arrival I broke down and shared with him the experience I had had after fervent prayer and eventually finding what I had been looking for.

Early in the afternoon we met up with the Manager of the jewelers who was very sympathetic to our situation and confirmed that a young man matching the description of our son had indeed brought the brooch in and was given a small sum of money in exchange.

However I was not allowed to buy it back there and then but was advised to bring in the owner of the brooch so she could then confirm that it was hers. If she identified it as her brooch it would then be returned in exchange for the amount previously paid to Paul.

I was very apprehensive at the difficult task ahead of me but I had no choice in the matter.

On returning home I retired to my bedroom and prayed for help that I might be given strength to explain the events of the last few days to my friend and that she would understand and forgive us. When I met up with her I broke down as I related to her the events of the last few days.

She quietly listened and put her arms around me and responded with love and forgiveness and agreed to meet the manager of the jewelers with me. When we arrived she identified the brooch as hers and it was returned for the sum of money originally paid to Paul. What a relief but also a very spiritual experience.

When we confronted Paul he was full of remorse and wrote a letter of apology to my friend for his conduct. She responded with love and forgave him. In a return letter she lovingly reminded him that his family loved him and cared for him and to understand how much he had hurt us all.

There would be many times when our patience would be tried and we would face many challenges as Paul continued to behave in ways that were upsetting and hurtful to me and the family.

One day he had gone to the local outdoor swimming pool in Gorleston and I received a telephone call from the lifeguard who enquired if I had a son by the name of "Paul". On confirming that I did he informed me that he was very drunk and could we collect him immediately? I was in shock. Where had Paul got alcohol from when he was under-age? I was soon to find out.

By now as I have shared with you we were living the Word of Wisdom and did not drink and would not normally have alcohol in the home. However, on this occasion, the French student who had been staying with us brought a bottle of wine and cheese as a gift from her parents. Not wishing to offend her we had put the wine away intending to dispose of it later but not soon enough to prevent our son from stealing it and drinking the entire contents.

IF ONLY I had thrown it away sooner.

The bottle of wine looked full and it wasn't until later on questioning Paul he confessed he had poured the wine into another bottle and filled the original with water to alley our suspicions. He was so ill. We left him to suffer with a hangover hoping he would learn the hard way and that would be the end of that. And suffer he did.

Was this the end of our troubles? Sadly it was just the beginning. Over a period of time several items went missing from the home. Toys, a watch, games, a drill, the yogurt maker, a high chair, money - the list was endless. All were taken at different times and not noticed until sometime later.

We had our suspicions but how can one know for certain that the one we suspected has committed the theft.

We decided to confront Paul but he was in denial and proving his guilt was extremely difficult.

I asked myself over and over again the same question. Why would Paul want to hurt us when we least deserved it? These things only happen to other people didn't they? We were just a normal family or so it seemed.

I felt so isolated, and because of my faith I felt so ashamed lest anyone should find out. How on earth was I going to be able to face everyone? How would my friends react? Would they understand or would they judge me?

The guilt set in. I started to blame myself for what had happened.

IF ONLY I hadn't had to move home so many times and Paul hadn't had to change school so often would life have taken a different path?

Chapter VIII - The Guilt Trip

"That I have great heaviness and continual sorrow in my heart"

KJV Romans 9:2

My husband and I felt upset, confused, withdrawn and desperately alone. I could only hope and pray that our son would eventually see the light and put his life in order. It was hard to comprehend that Paul would ever be dishonest; it was completely out of character as he, from a young age, had always been someone who could be trusted.

Paul used to love to play Monopoly with his older sister Karen and one day as they were engrossed in the game the phone rang, and while Karen left the room to answer it, Paul decided to cheat. But his conscience got the better of him and when she came back he confessed to what he had done.

He was such a lovely child and I felt so proud of him in every way.

Karen who by this time had just turned nineteen years old had met a very nice young man, Mark. Although not a member of the Church, he was receptive to the things that Karen shared with him about the gospel. Unfortunately, his mother didn't share in his enthusiasm and on finding out Mark was going out with our daughter exclaimed, 'Do you know she's a Mormon?' She was concerned as she had heard some untruths about the religion and was naturally wary. I remember she had thrown his scriptures across the room and insisted he returned them to us.

In those days The Book of Mormon was red and there were visible signs on the walls where the book had landed. But Mark was taught, accepted the gospel and was baptised. Later he decided to serve a mission for the Church and was called to serve in Denver, Colorado, USA.

Looking back I can fully understand how difficult this must have been for his parents.

He was in full- time employment and I am sure it was a time of testing and great sacrifice. He had to leave the company plus expect his parents to support his decision. This was particularly hard considering they were not Church members and during his two years away from home would be expected to support him emotionally.

Seeing Mark off on his mission was a new experience for us and like all families who prepare to say goodbye to a loved one it was exciting but stressful. We were proud and happy but also apprehensive as were his parents, and they not understanding or knowing the true principles of the gospel found it very difficult.

On the day of his departure we hired a minibus and invited Paul to travel with us all but he was reluctant and became rebellious towards the spiritual aspect of the faith. We felt overwhelmed with the whole experience. We struggled with our emotions at times as we tried to support Mark and also had to face the many challenges of a wayward son who was indifferent to the gospel.

We travelled to the airport and said a sad (but happy) goodbye to Mark and I remember feeling very disappointed that Paul had missed a very special family day where we could all have felt united and proud to see such a special young man choose to serve the Lord for two years.

IF ONLY the situation could have been different as I know how difficult it was for our daughter Karen saying goodbye to Mark. Perhaps she also sensed the tension we were all feeling knowing that he was leaving for two years and the disapproval of his parents. I was wishing Paul had joined us and Mark's family were more receptive to the gospel.

But he had a wonderful Mission in Colorado and served honorably, and had many conversions and baptisms which lifted our spirits and strengthened our testimonies.

Mark's mission and our friendship with his parents would bless us in the future when his mother and brother would also accept baptism. She became the Ward organist and to this day serves faithfully in this calling.

Mark's father Claude sadly did not accept but certainly softened his heart before his death and had great respect for us all. I remember visiting him in hospital shortly before he died and Mick asked if we could share a prayer with him and to our surprise he responded, 'Yes please, and I would like to give it if I can.'

The prayer Claude gave was beautiful and private and it was obvious he believed in Christ and his heart had been softened over the years. Both Mick and I had tears in our eyes as we left the hospital. Claude passed away just a few days later.

Following this successful mission, Mark and Karen were married and we now have three grandchildren: Katherine, John and Rachel.

Paul attended the wedding but we could see he was completely out of his comfort zone and his countenance had changed. But it was good to have him join us on this very special occasion.

By this time Paul who was sixteen years old had left school with little to show for it. He seemed to have little motivation, found it hard to find employment, and became very despondent. Life on benefits was not fun and there was little opportunity for him to be able to afford or enjoy the things that most teenagers like to indulge in.

Smoking was one habit that he and his friends dabbled in, and although we had banned it from the home, he spent most of his leisure time with a couple of lads who seemed on the surface very polite and good mannered and whose parents were very refined and had good homes.

Family photograph at our daughter's wedding. Rear from left to right Julie, Mick, Karen, me, Paul. Front Mark, Simon. My Dad is looking on

We were not overly concerned at that time and his friends would often come to our home and spend time with Paul. Sadly unbeknown to us and their parents, Paul and his friends were starting to experiment in drugs. I must strongly stress that we still had no idea at this point.

Many things came to light later and sometimes years later when I was given permission to read the reports on Paul written by the medical team who had attended to him.

What I read was to say the least, shocking. Paul was by then addicted to heroin and other drugs but we had no idea back then.

One evening when Paul had gone out with a friend he was later than usual arriving home and I contacted the other young man's another parents who was also concerned their son had not returned home on time either.

We met up and together we drove around the area and local country lanes and eventually found the police talking to them and giving them some advice and warnings. From the police we learned that several youth were meeting at a disused RAF Radar station.

The police had given them a verbal warning to stay away from the area but decided to take no further action.

I insisted on being taken to the radar station which required walking through some fields in pitch blackness. Fortunately we had a torch and on arriving at the place which was underground we were shocked at the sight that confronted us. The smell was repugnant, empty cans, discarded cigarette ends and other rubbish, and a feeling that I had entered a den of iniquity.

Is this where my son has been hanging out? What had been going on here? The mind boggled.

We had no proof that he was doing anything wrong of a serious nature but as parents felt we had to take action to prevent further worry for us all. We banned him from going out and punished him by withdrawing the companionship of his friends for a time. In short he was grounded.

Did this stop him? Not a bit. It only caused him to be more rebellious and stubborn. And life became very difficult in the home. This was my little bit of heaven on earth and now it was a place of conflict and upheaval.

So often parents are made to feel responsible for whatever goes wrong with their children. Before they judge, however, they should try wearing someone else's shoes. They would think differently before judging others.

I have read and listened to so many people who not having experienced the same situations as others seem to think they did it all right and everyone else have failed.

But I have learned so much from my own challenges. Now, I truly empathise with others who feel isolated by such heartache.

Most people think that rebellious youths come from broken homes or are a product of parents who have been too strict and or too lenient. Was I too strict or was I too lenient? How many parents will be asking that same question as they face the same challenges with their loved ones?

We were very sad and upset that Paul was smoking especially at a young age but there was little we could do to stop him. We had no idea at that time that there might be something more dangerous to worry about.

Smoking was enough for me to worry about because I know that smoking is addictive and addiction is a disease that can affect all families, the rich the poor, the good and the bad, those with strong faiths and those who have no faith. No one is exempt.

I have seen the terrible effects of those addicted to smoking.

I once read that:

'No one starts out hoping to be a drug addict, they just like drugs.'

'No one starts out hoping for a heart attack, they just like fried chicken.'

They find it hard to look ahead and see the consequences of their actions. And so it was with Paul. We were very upset that he was smoking but there was little we could do to stop him.

Most of us have made mistakes in our youth but we do not realise at the time how stupid we have been. It has been the way of life from the beginning of time. It is all part of life's experiences.

At least smoking seemed the lesser sin than dabbling in other more dangerous addictions. I had no understanding of drugs at the time and found it hard to recognise any signs in my son that were out of the ordinary. To me Paul was going through a difficult time in his teen years and, like most parents, I thought he would grow out of it and all would be well. But inside I was in turmoil.

Sleep did not come easily. Night after night I tossed and turned, crying and praying to God, seeking guidance and help to know what I should do for my son who I loved so much. I was consumed with worry.

But I also knew I had to take care of myself for the sake of my family and stay strong **IF ONLY** on the outside. Time passed with Paul becoming more distant and spending more and more time away from home.

Looking back, life then was very different as far as keeping contact was concerned. There were no mobile phones, no way of contacting him if he was late, no way of knowing where he was. The only way was to go to the places where he might possibly be and hopefully find him and bring him home.

But the older Paul became the more difficult it was. He was old enough to make decisions for himself but sadly they were not always wise ones.

All I had wanted was for my son to "choose the right" and put his life in order. Of course I felt proud as any mother does when her child is a credit to them. So many times when my heart had been full to bursting as I watched him sing with the youth, give talks and serve in the Church. One day he was assigned to speak in Sacrament on Spiritual and Physical Fitness and the pride I felt as he stood and gave a confident talk which would make any mother proud.

There were many happy times when everything seemed to be fine and we had so many family fun evenings and outings and memories that warmed my heart and touched my spirit.

I wanted it to last forever. What mother doesn't?

I loved my role as a mother and my whole life centered on being the best Mum I could.

A career could wait; the most important role I could play was to be there for my children and help them grow into fine adults themselves and eventually be good parents too.

To me motherhood is one of the greatest gifts given and the whole experience of carrying a child, giving birth and feeling somehow a closeness to God even amidst the pain is something I would not trade for anything.

It is a powerful connection between mother and child that is hard to describe. Not everyone will experience this as not all are naturally maternal but for me it is a God given gift for those of us blessed to have children. Whenever I think of birth it is a miracle that is hard for me to comprehend.

I believe with all my heart there is a God and there is far more to this life than we can ever envisage. And our time here is a proving time to prepare us for the next life. I hope I do not let my Savior down.

Chapter IX - Leaving Home

"My precious son wherever your journey in life may take you, I pray you will always be safe and never forget your way back home."

Author Unknown

Paul loved us so much but wanted his freedom and living at home was too restrictive for him. We were living our faith, and although Paul embraced it for years, the pull of the outside world was more appealing to him. It was with sadness and a heavy heart that I had to let my son go and find his way elsewhere.

I felt so helpless and could not accept that he would want to leave a loving home and family and give up so much for so little, but he was determined. This is what he wanted and he moved into a bedsit, and for a time he was keeping occasional contact and visited for meals, doing his laundry and sharing family times with us.

We felt our best solution was to: love him back; show him that family life was the best way to live; and this is where we wanted him to be.

During this time we maintained a reasonably normal relationship. Inwardly my heart ached to have him home with us where I could see him on a regular basis. Secretly, I hoped, with time and with us setting him a good example, he would turn his life around.

I was serving in the Church at the time as Primary President. Although I outwardly appeared to be coping, I sometimes felt overwhelmed as I tried to juggle with challenges in the home, fulfill my callings, and care for our family while Mick was working offshore. Although overwhelmed with life's challenges I did enjoy my Church callings because I knew I had been called through prayer before the call was extended to me.

All callings are given following prayer by our Bishop and his counselors and I have managed to fulfill them all with the Lords help.

I have held many callings over the years: Stake Relief Society, Young Women and Primary, Ward Relief Society, Young Women and Primary. I have also served as a Seminary Teacher, Fundraising Chairman, Spiritual Living Teacher in Relief Society, Secretary, Missionary, Single Adult Board member and a Teacher in Relief Society, Primary and Sunday school.

I never envisioned I would one day be considered capable of fulfilling such tasks since I had neither the experience nor the confidence. Looking back over my life, I remember my father was not one to compliment anyone on their accomplishments. This no doubt hurt my self-esteem in later years.

I remember telling him I was going to learn to drive, and being an older woman at the time he quickly responded, 'You? You'll never cope with driving on the roads these days.'

No encouraging words were ever spoken.

Those comments were like a red rag to a bull.

I quietly thought, 'Well, we will see.'

It took a year, but to my surprise and joy, I passed my driving test first time.

I went on to take a computer course and passed first time. I also applied for a nursing job in the hospital and was accepted at the interview. Looking back, I was hired for every job I applied for.

As the saying goes, *you have never failed until you have stopped trying.*

Serving in so many different areas in the Church had been a great morale booster for me. I know that God does not always call the qualified, but he does qualify the called.

With his help, I have been able to achieve much. I grew by serving and giving my all to whatever the Lord had in store for me, and I know the Holy Ghost has prompted me on so many occasions.

I cannot over emphasise the wonderful gift the Holy Ghost is to me, It had guided me given me answers to prayers and even warned me of impending danger.

I remember vividly as Primary President praying for a

pianist and receiving the answer I was not expecting. The sister had recently returned to Church after many years following a near-fatal car accident and she was confined to a wheelchair. I put forward her name with faith that it was the right decision and waited for further confirmation from the Bishop. He prayerfully considered her and concluded that this was an inspired call. He then interviewed the sister and extended the calling to her. She explained that her accident caused her to lose co-ordination between her hands. In short, she couldn't play.

Bishop looked her straight in the eyes and said, 'But the Lord has called you.' She responded, 'Then I will give it a try.' She accepted the calling and said she would give her best but could not promise anything.

She struggled for quite some time, but through perseverance and a lot of help and encouragement, she eventually overcame the problem and became proficient enough to become the Ward organist and Choir leader. Under her leadership the Gorleston Ward Choir excelled and came first in a Stake Choir competition.

I learned a great lesson from that experience. Be very prayerful and the Lord will direct your path.

The organist we have today had not played since she was a child and struggled to carry out her calling. To even play one simple hymn, she had to spend many hours in quiet solo practice in the chapel, but to date she is still the organist. She still maintains it is a struggle to come up to the standard she would like but is dedicated to her calling. God moves in mysterious ways.

My life was so very busy, but I am who I am today because I tried to forget my challenges and lose myself in service to others.

But worrying about Paul did not make life easy, as I tried to live the gospel and cope with the challenges of a rebellious son. I found it hard to accept the decision he had made to turn away from all that was important to me.

As a child, Paul did not have good eating habits unlike the rest of the family, and I had become quite concerned about this especially during his teen years.

I decided to get advice from my doctor. He asked whether Paul had any current health problems relating to his eating and I said he did not. The doctor then replied, 'Well what's your problem then?'

But years later Paul's poor diet would have a profound effect on his health.

Over time he became very pale and withdrawn. He grew his hair longer, and did not take care of it. It was greasy, and looked as though he had not washed it for some time. His skin became very spotty, and he appeared generally undernourished, but I was still unaware that this might be serious at the time. Maybe I did have my suspicions, but I did not want to acknowledge the fact. I really don't know.

He became so different to the lovely boy we once knew.

I do remember on occasions searching his pockets, smelling his clothes and trying to find any sign that would help me to establish whether or not Paul was dabbling in something more serious than smoking.

But it was easier to bury my head in the sand than to confront my son and ask whether he might be taking drugs. I just could not face it.

A photograph of Paul in his flat

IF ONLY I could have understood more clearly and recognised the signs.

Maybe I was in denial and just could not accept it. It was unthinkable. These things happened to other people, didn't they?

Knowing of others who had become addicted to drugs my heart went out to them. I could see the effect it was having on their families and I couldn't imagine how I would have felt in their position.

Sometime later I heard of a young girl who was addicted to drugs. There was a picture of her tragic death as she lay in a seedy bedsit with obvious signs of her drug taking. The image even showed the needle still in her arm.

This is how her parents had found her, and the mother had wanted the world to see the picture. She wanted to warn others of the tragedy of taking illegal drugs and the consequences, not only for the daughter but for the whole family.

They were a loving family with a comfortable home but they had no idea their daughter had got caught up in the drug scene until it was too late.

I felt great compassion for them and grieved for their loss of a much loved daughter.

There are so many stories of grief and sadness, some well-known, others just ordinary people who for one reason or another turned to drugs. They may have fallen under the influence of their peers, and others perhaps succumbed to the devastating results of drug addiction.

Would these parents ever get over the torment as they grieved for their beautiful child who had everything to live for? I didn't think so.

There have been so many other instances since then that have come to light through the media, and my heart has gone out to them all in their pain and sorrow.

A father was so distraught at the loss of his son to drugs and so consumed with grief, he went to the house of the young man who he felt was responsible for his son's death. He stabbed him to death than hung himself. Such was his overwhelming feelings of loss at the untimely death of his son.

There are so many sad and pointless deaths, and so many broken and devastated families wondering "how and why" such a tragedy could have happened to them.

Comparing myself to them at the time, my challenges seemed to fade into insignificance. Although Paul was smoking and addicted, it could have been so much worse. Or so I thought.

Time would tell.

In 1983, Mick was called to an interview at Norwich Stake

along with other Priesthood holders. Following the interview, he was asked to wait outside as they might want to see him again. He was later called in and was extended the call of High Councilman. The Stake President said, 'As ordinary men we would not call you to this position, as we don't know how you will be able to fulfill the calling. You work offshore up to six months a year, you don't have a car or telephone, but the Lord has called you.' Mick said he felt a warm feeling come over him and when the Stake President asked, 'Will you accept the calling?'

Mick gladly accepted and then spent the next six weeks away on a couple of projects. How would he be able to work offshore and fulfill his new calling? Well God works in mysterious ways and after much pondering and prayer, Mick felt prompted to approach his employer and request an office job explaining to him the need to spend more time with his family.

He had never worked in an office and began to wonder if he had made the right decision.

When Mick was thirteen years of age he ran away because he was so unhappy at home. He had not been treated well by his stepfather and life became unbearable. . With the help of a children's association, he was offered a place on the *Arethusa*, a boys' training ship in Kent, where he spent two years. He then joined the Royal Navy at the age of fifteen and travelled the world for the next twelve years. After leaving the navy he got a job working for an offshore commercial survey company. From a young age, life at sea was all Mick had known.

Mick wrote the following poem that illustrates his optimism on life no matter what it throws at you.

You Ran Away to Get Away

You ran away to get away
But found that life is not that way
For love can find a better way
For someone's life from day to day

To leave one's mother and siblings
Is hard enough for both those things

But when you do, it also brings
An adventurous life on eagle's wings

For you can fly, high in the sky
And overcome that fear and shy
And see below what you can try
Then go and do, go on and apply

Life's trials are the best
Don't linger and take rest
For life is also one big test
To see if you can, become the best

No matter what it throws at you
Remember what you're going through
Life's trials that will hitherto
Make a boy a man of you

So don't despair at what you find
For you are not so dumb or blind
Cos love will give you peace of mind
And help you be so more refined

In all of this there is much fun
But don't forget you're lovely Mum
Who brought you up as her eldest son
And God will reward you when life is done

For you will be with her once more
When you decide to come ashore
And pass beyond the veil's door
And your love for her you will outpour
Once more

Michael Colley

It was not an easy decision for him, but he knew changes had to be made if he was to fulfil his calling and spend more time at home.

He was offered a job in the office working in the marketing department with a requirement to work up to 6 weeks a year offshore but he would also be required go away on occasional day trips visiting clients. What a miracle. The Lord had paved the way for him once again.

Nine months later, Mick attended one of his High Council Meetings. While there he was interviewed by the Stake President once again and extended the call of Bishop of the Gorleston Ward. The High Council sustained him as a Bishop at the meeting that evening.

On returning home that night, he sat me down and told me of his new calling, but I already knew in my heart and proceeded to relate to him the following experience:

While I was working in the kitchen one day during last October I had a vision of you presiding as the Bishop of the Ward and then the vision vanished.

Mick then related to me that he also knew in October that he would be called as a Bishop for it was also revealed to him.

Mick's calling as Bishop came just nine months after being called as a High Councilman and by this time, we did have a car and telephone.

The way ahead was being prepared for him to fulfil this new calling as Bishop.

What an experience. It is at times like these that one's faith is strengthened. Mick served as Bishop for almost six years after he was sustained by the Ward Members. It is a demanding calling, but he was a good Bishop and gave his all. He never murmured and was so kind, compassionate and loved the members. He also always set aside special times for his family. As well as serving as Bishop, Mick had to travel away from home sometimes, but somehow with the help of good Counselors, he was able to fulfil his duties.

For those who may one day read my story, Bishops, unlike many other religions, do not receive payment and have to work during the day and dedicate what time they can to their flock.

There are many lonely hours for a Bishop's wife and his family.

I remember someone saying to me one day, 'Sometimes we are separated in this life to be together in the next.'

I hope and pray that is true because there have been many times throughout the years when we have been separated through work, family commitments and Church.

One day our youngest son was asked to give a talk on Service in the Sacrament Service, and he wrote the following poem:

My Dad's a Bishop

When I was only very young
And didn't understand
My Dad was called as Bishop
I thought it was quite grand.

I didn't really realise how busy he would be
And we would see him now and then
When he would stop for tea
He'd go off to his meetings
And I would feel quite sad
Because I'd want him home with me
To be my special Dad

We'd plan to do some nice things
Like swimming, football too
And then he'd say "I'm sorry son
I've got a lot to do"

Although he hasn't many days
When he can share with me
I'm glad my Dad's a Bishop
Because I now can see

He's taught me how to pray
And be as good as I can be
To love my friends and neighbour's
And all my family

And if I grow up faithful
And do the best that I can do
He's told me we can be together
Mum, brothers, sisters too

It may not be in this life
For we have to do our best
And work and serve each other
For life is just a test

To see if we are faithful
And will give up lots of time
To serve the Lord and love Him
Just like that Dad of mine

One day I'll have my Dad at home
And we will share once more
The things he missed so often
When he was Bishop of our Ward

I know he loves his calling
And loves to serve you too
So I'm glad my Dad's a Bishop
And I hope that you are too.

Simon Colley

I remember one Sunday following the Sacrament service finding him sitting outside the Bishop's office. On asking him why he was waiting there he said, 'I am waiting to have an interview with my Dad like the others are doing.' Mick kindly spent a few minutes with him and Simon came away beaming.

We may not have had *quantity* time but we did have *quality* time and many wonderful and happy times were spent together as a family.

Everyone has challenges in their lives and so it was for us but I was not prepared for what was about to happen next. Paul was visiting with us for a meal and to do his laundry. He looked very ill and appeared agitated and seemed to be slurring his words. We left him to eat his lunch and retired to the lounge. When I returned to the dining room, I found Paul slumped over his food, then trying to raise his head only to slump forward again.

I tried to communicate with him, but he seemed unable to hold a conversation. I hurried to my husband asked him to come and see for himself how Paul was behaving.

He spoke to Paul and asked him a few questions to try and get some information from him, but it was difficult to ascertain what was causing Paul to act in this way.

At that point Mick asked Paul to roll up his sleeves. He was in no fit state to comply but Mick insisted and our worst fears were confirmed. We saw what appeared to be needle marks covering both arms.

I broke down in tears and felt sick to know that Mick's suspicions had been confirmed and my son, my precious son, was taking drugs.

We counselled and pleaded with him to turn away from such a terrible existence and told him we would help him all that we could to fight the cravings that had now taken over his life. I told him how much I loved him and wanted him to have a future. A future where he could make something good with his life and feel proud of his achievements.

I slumped back in my chair waiting for a response, anything, but was met with silence and indifference. If we were expecting an admittance of guilt, we would not be getting it that evening.

The atmosphere was charged and somber, as we pleaded with Paul and begged him to listen to us. We told him **IF ONLY** he would see the error of his ways; we would help and support him to change his life for the better. It was to no avail, and he left home to go back to his place shortly afterwards. This would be the beginning of long absences when no contact was made and we were left not knowing how he was surviving or if he was surviving at all.

We had offered to help in any way we could, but by now Paul was over twenty-one, a man, and nothing we suggested could persuade him to listen and accept help from anyone. He chose to be left alone.

It was so hard not knowing how he was doing. Was he ok? Where had he moved to?

It was difficult to trace him. So many thoughts go through your mind, and not knowing the best way to help your own son is frustrating. Especially knowing that unless he accepted our support, things wouldn't change except he was willing to put forth the effort.

I remember one occasion when we decided to visit Paul after we had successfully traced his then present address. My first impression was of absolute shock and dismay.

We were shown into the house by the owner of the property, which was split into several rooms. The condition of Paul's apartment was shocking, and to make matters worse, we were told that Paul had disappeared without a forwarding address.

I was shaken by what I had seen. The room had no windows and was in an appalling condition. It was dark and depressing and very foreboding. It is hard to put into words my shock when I first entered the room. I felt so very vulnerable and afraid. I would not have wanted an animal to live in such conditions, let alone my son.

It was obvious that others in the building were on drugs, and I truly felt afraid and desperately wanted to leave and run away from the whole situation. This would be the beginning of many moves over the years. It was often weeks and even months that Paul would go missing which would leave us worried about his safety and wellbeing.

Time passed. Visits were spasmodic but very welcome when Paul did make the effort to contact us.

He would turn up out of the blue and choose to share a meal with us, and we would sit and reason with him for hours. We would share our concerns, our love for him and our hope that he would see the error of his ways and make a determined effort to turn away from the life he was living. It wasn't even a life, but an existence, and one that would destroy him if he carried on the way he was going.

On one evening together, Mick asked Paul if he would be interested in a job. There was a possibility that he might be able to get him some work with a shipping company working offshore. This suggestion was warmly received by Paul, much to our relief. Mick set up the appointment for him.

I saw a light at the end of the tunnel and prayed this would help Paul to turn his life around and find a meaning to his existence.

Chapter X - All at Sea

"Reach for new harbours through different phases of life.
Make memories and enjoy your journey".

Author Unknown

The interview went well and Paul commenced work within the week. It is hard to put into words how I felt, to know that my son had at last been offered employment and outwardly seemed happier.

He seemed to have settled in well and travelled to faraway places. But we had little idea that Paul had become unhappy and was treated badly by some of those onboard. But he determined to persevere, and he stayed with the company for two years.

Then one day he called sounding very distressed saying he could not take the job anymore. It appeared that over a period of time, some of those on the ship had bullied him, made homosexual advances to him, and threatened him as to what they were going to do to him.

This was the last straw for him, and he said he'd had enough. We told him we understood, would be with him as soon as possible, and the matter would be reported to the company.

It was devastating to see the pain on Paul's face. He had tried so hard to keep this job down, and now, he was thrown back once again with the possibility of unemployment. We tried to calm the situation and temporarily settled Paul at home with us.

The matter was reported by Mick to the shipping company manager who had employed Paul. Sadly, the response was completely lacking in compassion or understanding. The only comment was that "these things happen when onboard a ship and little could be done about it". That was it. Of course, things would be different now and the perpetrators would have faced the consequences of their actions.

And so Paul faced life on the dole once again.

He slipped back into depression and became very distant and wanted to be left alone. We had come to accept this as Paul was a mature man now and we respected his need for privacy. He knew how much we loved him, and we assured him we would always be there for him.

During these years, we had no idea as to what drugs Paul was taking. It would be years before everything came to light as to the full extent of his addiction.

One day Paul contacted us and informed us he had been offered a council flat. He sounded so happy and relieved to have a home of his home at last, and we shared in his joy.

At least we would know where he was and that he had a place fit to live in. Once again life seemed a little less stressful and some pressure, thankfully, was taken off us

Our sons, Mark and Simon, were at this time attending karate, and Paul decided to join them. He appeared fitter and happier than we had seen him for years. We prayed that this was the end of what had been a living nightmare.

He now had a new home and a desire to get fit. I cannot express how relieved and happy I felt to know my son at last wanted to turn his life around.

He applied for a job in a factory and was successful in getting the employment he wanted. He continued positively and put his heart into the work, which although repetitive and boring, gave him a reason for living once again.

We were so proud that he was determined to do his best even though he had to rise at 4:30am each day.

Over time, he was promoted to charge hand and this helped so much to build his self- esteem.

But our joy was short-lived.

We received a phone call from Paul who sounded in distress. He told us there had been a fire in his flat while he was at work, and the fire brigade and police had been called. The fire had been extinguished, but he was left with nothing but blackened and charred damage.

Mick and I arrived at the scene and were once again shocked at the sight facing us. We assessed the damage caused not so much by the fire itself but by the smoke. I thought my heart would break.

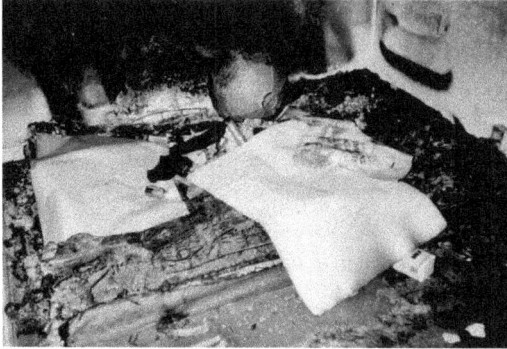

Photograph of Paul's burnt bed completely destroyed.

Anyone who has experienced the trauma of a fire in the home will understand the devastation that confronted us that day. The bed was ash and cinders, and everything within sight was destroyed or beyond recognition.

It seemed the fire was started by either a faulty electric blanket being left on or by a smoldering cigarette.

Whatever the cause, it was insignificant at the time. Cleaning up was our priority.

How on earth does one begin the task of cleaning up such and awful mess? I had never witnessed anything like it. No words can describe the emotions we felt to see what once was a very nice flat almost destroyed. It was devastating.

Mick and I, our daughter Julie and our youngest son Simon set to, with help from Paul. It was a painstaking task with the smell of smoke permeating everything including ourselves.

It was heartbreaking and almost more than we could bear.

Days were spent restoring the flat to a livable condition to enable Paul to move back and settle in once again. In the meantime, he temporarily moved back home with us.

We had contacted the council, but they had made it clear that Paul would be responsible for the cleanup if he was to continue living there as a tenant. Some of the floorboards were burnt, but they refused to repair or replace them. There was no empathy whatsoever. Just indifference.

But at least Paul was alive when the end result could have been so very serious, and one I did not want to contemplate.

Words can't describe the feelings and thoughts during the following few weeks. I constantly worried as to how this had happened. Was Paul under the influence of drugs or was it a pure accident?

I was to learn years later, when reading his medical report, that Paul was free from drugs for three years when working at the factory. So, I can only assume that it was an accident.

What was of most importance was Paul was safe, and the residents each side were unaffected by the fire. It was great relief to us all.

After the cleanup and replacing the destroyed items, and with the help of friends who quietly donated necessary bedding and money, we were able to settle Paul back into his home once again. He appeared to be so much happier now that he was back in his home once again. He met a young woman working at the same factory. She brought Paul the happiness he was looking for. Sadly they split up within a year and this devastated Paul. But he continued to work in the same department and somehow managed to perform well in his job.

All seemed well and Paul gave everything he had to his job, and enjoyed the responsibility he had been given.

Looking back this was probably the best time of his adult life, not perfect by any means and not the career of his choice, but on the positive side, he was earning a decent wage and was respected enough to be given promotion.

I must add that during these tumultuous years Paul never denied the Church.

He had read The Book of Mormon more than once and talked to others about the Church and our involvement in it.

Mick was a Bishop for nearly six years at this point, and Paul was not afraid to share this with others.

A year after Mick had been called, Paul asked if he could bring some friends around to talk about the Church. We were overjoyed to know that he still had respect for the gospel and wanted to share it with others. Paul's friend, Chris, brought his girlfriend, Anna, with him and we had a wonderful evening talking and sharing the film "Man's Search for Happiness" with them.

We were bombarded with questions, and they left feeling uplifted and happy as was Paul. But it would be quite some time before we saw the results of that missionary evening.

Anna attended Church on occasions, and eventually she was baptised. There was a very special spirit which brought many to tears, and it was wonderful to see Paul feeling the spirit too. She attended Relief Society evenings with me and started to take an active part in the Church.

I was a missionary at this time, and I felt my cup was overflowing.

But it was with great sadness that we later learned her relationship had broken up and   she had moved away. Sadly we lost contact with her. Some of Paul's friends moved away without our knowledge too with no forwarding address, but one day a letter arrived from Chris one of his friends informing us he was working offshore on the rigs and could we send him the book "Jesus the Christ" to read. It was wonderful to know he still had feelings for the gospel and had a desire to study.

I wrote back to him expressing my joy at hearing from him once again and hoped he would enjoy read the book prayerfully. I also shared my testimony with him and asked him to keep in touch with us, but that was the last we heard from him I'm sad to say.

I was unable to contact him although I tried.

Meanwhile, Paul continued to dedicate himself to work, and life was more tranquil for all. There was still such relief and joy to see such a change in him. But being a Mum, I still inwardly worried that he would relapse and distance himself from the family again. But I counted my blessings and thanked my Heavenly Father for the return of my son who was lost but was found.

Chapter XI - The Prodigal Son Returns

"I love you not because I need you; I need you because I love you."

Author Unknown

But my joy was short-lived. Paul rang one day to say he had lost his job.

It appears form the information I gained later that an employee continually taunted Paul and gave him a very hard time. Paul restrained himself for as long as he could, but eventually he verbally retaliated.

The man was furious and lunged at Paul punching him in the face. Sadly Paul lost control and hit back. The result was instant dismissal for both of them.

This was devastating and a great setback for him and us. Once again, he sank into depression, and as we learned years later, he went back onto drugs.

So began a vicious circle and a time of great sadness, as he reverted back to his old lifestyle.

The visits to us became less frequent and as much as we tried to help Paul, he distanced himself. There were long absences and no one could reach him and convince him he was travelling a rocky path once again - throwing away the wonderful progress he had made. During this time Paul was taken to court many times and had to face the consequences of his actions.

Below are just a few examples.

- Possessing a controlled drug. 12 months' probation and 100 hours community service.
- Theft and possessing a controlled drug. Community

 service
- Script date altered plus stolen cheque book. Community service
- Shoplifting
- Stock lifting
- Theft and shoplifting
- Controlled drug usage
- Controlled drug usage

And the list goes on.

These were difficult times.

If a loved one becomes an addict, the effects are far reaching. The whole family suffers, and therefore I feel reluctant to go too deeply into personal details of the years and pain and sorrow we felt, as we saw our son's life spiral out of control.

One day Paul appealed to his sister to lend him money as those he owed it to had threatened to break his legs if he didn't pay up.

It was with a heavy heart that she refused him. To this day, she remembers Paul sitting outside on a wall, head in his hands, and obviously in despair.

He then went to his other sister who reluctantly did give him some money with a heavy heart not knowing if it might be spent on drugs. Sometimes difficult decisions have to be made, and over the years we came to realise this. But it is hard nevertheless.

Tough love or unconditional love?

I have seen sad results from both sides of the equation.

Only those who have experienced the pain of a loved one addicted to drugs can fully understand how difficult it is to make decisions when confronted with the alternative.

- If I refuse to help, what will be the outcome?
- Will he end up dead?
- If he did, would I ever forgive myself?
- Could I have done more?
- On the other hand, if I am too lenient will the outcome be the same?

To this day, I do not have the answers to these questions.

I remember one occasion Paul and his sister visited their biological father in Plymouth. Paul had left a used needle in the bathroom, and blood was found on the floor. His father was distressed and felt helpless.

He was not used to coping with the situation since he only saw Paul on very rare occasions due to distance, and financial circumstances

He too must have thought, **IF ONLY** he could help Paul. As my former husband also concluded, Paul was a grown man and trying to help someone who is not ready to be helped is difficult.

At that time, Paul was on methadone which enabled him to cope. He was trying to wean himself off the harder drugs, and it was a very upsetting period for them all and spoiled what was intended to be a special family time for them all.

There were many distressing times ahead. It was hard to deal with the pain and sorrow that we felt to see the depths to which Paul had plummeted.

There was occasional contact when we had some special events taking place. One of these times was the baptism of our son Mark's girlfriend. Paul attended and we had a wonderful evening together. I felt happy and elated sharing this happy occasion together.

Shortly afterwards, Mark left on a mission to Leeds. Paul was invited to travel down to the London Mission Home to say goodbye, but he failed to turn up. He did however write some lovely letters to Mark while he was away.

The following are some excerpts from some of those letters:

I want you to know that I love you and my family very much even if it may seem as if I couldn't care less a lot of the time. I wonder why you all keep caring for me when all I do is cause worry and pain.

I hope that one day soon my life will find a direction and a future to look forward to and I will then have a chance at being a decent brother and son like the one my family so richly deserve.

I found it really emotional watching the video of the day you left and felt really sad. Now you are away for two years, I feel really choked. I so regret not having said goodbye and even though you may forgive me, I cannot forgive myself.

I am sure all the family are missing you but especially Mum. They tend to worry more than others and think more about every situation and emotion their child may be experiencing. They will lie awake at night churning it all around feeling intense emotions and worry.

I know this is true because I have probably caused Mum to worry more than most but never understood it when I was young.

Every time you are persecuted in your work for Christ, remember he gave his life for you.

These are just a few of the wonderful words written by Paul to his missionary brother. They reflect the special person he was and how he loved his family. They also show the remorse he felt at some of his actions.

Following his mission Mark married his girlfriend, but Paul had distanced himself once again and sadly did not attend the wedding.

From their union we have three grandchildren: Joshua, Lawson and Marcus.

Our family took part in the Church events, and Paul did attend some of them. He seemed to enjoy them most of the time, but he did struggle to fit in. He found it all a little overwhelming at times, but I was just grateful to have him there beside us.

During this time, our daughter Julie had met a returned missionary. We were pleased and happy to know that after the many challenges she had over the years, she had at last found someone who would care and love her.

She had sadly strayed from the teachings of the Church when in her teens, and her life had taken a different direction when she fell in love with a young man with different standards. Although we had a love for him, it was not an ideal situation, and he was not the right one for her. Many years later she made the decision to return to Church, turn her life around and put the things of the world behind her. Sadly, she left her boyfriend after many years together.

This was a very difficult decision knowing there were few suitable and eligible young men available.

Family photograph inside the chapel following the wedding ceremony. Paul is on the left next to his sister Karen. Mark is not present as he was serving a Church mission in Leeds.

Life became a struggle for her. It was hard to witness the sadness at times as she did her very best to live the gospel, fulfill her callings and battle with ill health. She had been diagnosed some years earlier with Myalgic Encephalomyelitis (ME) following a severe bout of glandular fever.

The wedding reception. Paul is surrounded by his nieces and one of his nephews.

Paul dancing with his sister Julie at her wedding.

To meet someone who was worthy and had just returned home having served an honorable two year mission was such a blessing to her, and within a few months they were married.

Paul attended the wedding, and we were overjoyed to have him join with us once again mingling with our friends and family. He looked well and more like the Paul we knew. I felt like my prodigal son had returned once again.

From the union of Kenny and Julie, we have three grandchildren: Sarah-Beth, Lewis and Joel.

Sadly my joy was short-lived. Paul distanced himself from us once again, and there followed a return of long absences when he chose to be left alone.

By now we recognised the signs. I believe Paul felt a lot of guilt when he attended Church, and although he was pleased for his siblings, nevertheless felt like a failure.

I have no doubt he quietly wanted what they had **IF ONLY** he could overcome his addictions. We never did anything to make him feel this way. We loved him unconditionally.

Chapter XII -
A Lonely Christmas

"A merry heart maketh a cheerful countenance: but
by sorrow of the heart the spirit is broken."

KJV Proverbs 15:13

Christmas was approaching. For many people, it can either be a time of great joy or sadness.

The thought of Paul being alone on Christmas Day caused me heartbreak, but I did my best to reach out and let him know I loved him.

My feelings were mixed. I did enjoy the spirit of Christmas and the bonding of family, but without our son Paul, it was never the same. But life had to go on. I made my preparations for the family and tried to find a few gifts for Paul in the hope he would be sharing it with us.

Just prior to Christmas, I was shopping in the local town and noticed a young man selling *The Big Issue* magazines. Although I had regularly purchased the magazine, I felt a particularly strong urge to buy one, but being in a hurry, I tried to put the thought to the back of my mind.

Again the feeling came over me, but I walked away again. Why was I being drawn to this young man? I assumed it was the Christmas spirit. My thoughts were constantly with those who were homeless and how sad I felt for them.

But again, I dismissed it from my mind and continued walking.

The third time the prompting came I turned back and approached the vendor, bought a magazine, and asked him a little about himself. I enquired how long he had been selling the magazine. Did he live locally? Did he find it hard standing for hours selling the *Big Issue* and find the majority of the public walk by?

During the conversation I learned that he knew Paul, and he wished so much he had somewhere to live like my son. He was hoping to better himself by selling the *Big Issue* magazine.

I wished him well and proceeded to make my way home. On my arrival I received a telephone call informing me my mother was very ill with pneumonia, and our family was very concerned for her.

Mick and I decided to travel down and be with her. We would have a quiet Christmas with Mum and Dad and help in any way we could.

Mum was indeed very ill, and we were very concerned for her. Thankfully she showed signs of improvement before we had to return back home and did eventually make a full recovery.

When we arrived back, I met with my daughter and shared with her the experience I had with the *Big Issue* vendor. I told her how I had felt particularly drawn to him that day until I could not ignore it and about my feelings of sadness at the plight of the homeless at Christmas. I expressed my wish to do more for them.

I shared how it had played on my mind more strongly than usual, but l couldn't think why at the time.

She listened quietly but said little in response. She enquired after her grandmother's condition and how our Christmas had been.

A few days later, having let Mick and I settle in at home, she sadly informed me that Paul had been evicted from his home while I was away. She couldn't bring herself to tell me when the incident happened. She knew the stress we were under with my mother's ill-health and decided to give us time to unwind before adding to our stress. .

She explained that Paul had been unable to pay his rent, and the bailiffs had gone in took possession of some items, and thrown the rest in a nearby garage. My son was now homeless.

Was this why I had been so strongly drawn to the *Big Issue* vendor and the plight of the homeless?

This news of Paul's eviction was especially heartrending for one family member who had taken out a loan to pay off Paul's accrued debts. We were not aware of this as they themselves had very little money. They so badly wanted for Paul to keep a roof over his head and had been willing to do this for him. We were only made aware of their generosity many years later.

I was numb with shock and enquired where we could find him.

It is hard to put into words the emotions I felt at the time. I was mentally and physically tired, and now had to face the shock of my son losing his home. What would the future hold for him?

When we were told Paul was sleeping on the floor at a friend's accommodation in less than desirable conditions, we immediately made our way to see how he was coping once again.

It was a very emotional reunion, but I assured him that we would support him and have him live with us until other arrangements could be made.

He showed us what was left of his belongings in a nearby garage, and we were shocked at the way the bailiffs had treated them. They had literally thrown his belongings on the floor, and in the process had broken and damaged several items.

Why did they need to do this?

I felt saddened and angry at those who have very little respect for others at times like this and treat them with such contempt. I felt devastated, sad and very angry. Why was it necessary just before Christmas?

We made our way home and tried to settle Paul in as best we could.

I wondered how this new living arrangement with him would work out. I was soon to find out. Paul became depressed and spent long hours away from home often arriving back in the early hours of the morning.

There were times when I wanted to quit trying. It was so hard, but the feelings never lasted for long and I would always pick myself up realising that I loved my son too much to turn my back on him.

The following poem has helped me often when life seems so dark and dreary:

Don't Quit

When things go wrong, as they sometimes will,
When the road you're trudging seems all uphill,
When funds are low and the debts are high,
And you want to smile but you have to sigh,
When care is pressing you down a bit,
Rest if you must, but don't you quit.

Life is queer with its twists and turns,
As every one of us sometimes learns,
And many a failure turns about,
When he might have won if he'd stuck it out.
Don't give up, though the pace seems slow -
You may succeed with another blow.

Often the goal is nearer than
It seems to a faint and faltering man;
Often the struggler has given up
When he might have captured the victor's cup,
And he learned too late, when the night slipped down,
How close he was to the golden crown.

Success is failure turned inside out -
The silver tint of the clouds of doubt,
And you never can tell how close you are -
It may be near when it seems afar;
So stick to the fight when you're hardest hit -
It's when things seem worst that you mustn't quit.

Author Unknown

In the weeks ahead, we spent many hours talking and counseling with Paul. We told him how much we loved him and wanted to help, but we also had house rules which we expected him to respectfully follow. We would not tolerate anything that would cause distress and contention within the family.

We tried to settle into a routine, and we all did our best to get along as a family unit. Paul seemed outwardly relieved and less depressed when we assured him that we truly loved him. Life was tranquil for a time, but it was to be short-lived.

During his time with us, we had reluctantly been looking after a snake belonging to Paul. One night I had left our youngest son, Simon, with Paul while I attended a Church meeting. On returning home I found him looking worried and upset.

He said, 'Paul has been on the floor on his knees sorting out his possessions very slowly, and organising them on the floor for ages. He keeps repeating the same procedure over and over again.

'He asked me who I was and who was looking after me. I went and hid in my bedroom and locked the door. Paul seemed like a stranger, and I was scared. He didn't seem to be in possession of his body. I saw a needle, and it really scared me.'

We tried to defuse the situation while our younger son was present, but privately made it clear to Paul that we would not tolerate any form of drug taking while he was in our home. I reiterated he would have to abide by the rules while living under our roof or find somewhere else to live.

We searched everywhere for the needle but were unsuccessful. To this day, we have no idea what happened to it.

I remember Paul's feeble explanation that the needle was a syringe to feed the snake. It was an excuse and one that fell on deaf ears, of course.

There were many ups and downs in the days that followed, but we were not expecting life to be a bed of roses.

But things came to a head in the early hours of one particular morning. We had retired to our bed at the usual time, but about 2am our smoke alarm in the hall downstairs went off waking us up.

We jumped out of bed expecting to see a fire, but on reaching the kitchen, we found Paul in a stupor leaning over a lit gas hob. He was wearing a hat that had caught fire, and he seemingly was unable to control the situation.

He appeared to be under the influence of drugs.

Mick quickly pulled the hat off Paul's head, poured water over it and put out the fire. By this time we were tired and weary, and we momentarily lost it verbally with Paul. We shouted at him telling him that we could not live our lives like this not knowing what would happen next. Not only was his life in danger, but our lives could be in danger too if Paul carried on the way he was going.

We waited for a response, but Paul was in no condition to account for his actions.

We assured him we would do all we could to help him to come off the drugs, but he needed to put forth the effort himself and want to change his life, which was spiraling out of control.

This was the last straw for me. By now I was overwhelmingly tired, and struggling to sleep, function and carry out my duties as a wife and mother. .

I have always had an aversion to confrontation which no doubt stems from my childhood but it was all too much. I had had enough.

I remember looking back over our early years in the Church and the joy I felt as we were taught "The Plan of Happiness" and then years later having moments of reflection and thinking to myself. *Is this it?* Is this "The Plan of happiness"?

All around me I witnessed those who were suffering throughout the world in so many different circumstances: ill health, homelessness, death, persecution, financial burdens earthquakes, suicide, divorce, abuse, bullying, hunger, and war. There were moments when through my own pain, I wondered whether I could endure. All seemed lost.

So many hours were spent in prayer and pleading for relief of so many but still the trials continued.

But I am thankful my faith has sustained me. and I do believe that there will be a "light at the end of the tunnel" for all if we can understand the plan more clearly and know that this life is a small part of eternity, and we can go on to better things in the life to come.

But we need to have faith in "spite of".

I know enduring to the end is the hard part but will be worth it, I am sure.

And so I carried on, convincing myself that things would get better if I kept setting the example and continue to love and show Paul a better way.

Chapter XIII - The Last Straw

"Do not worry if you feel low; the sun has a sinking spell every night, but rises again the next morning."

Author Unknown

Mick's work required him to spend some periods away from home, but he always did his utmost to support me. It was very stressful for him, too, trying to fulfill his role as a husband, father and Bishop. I am eternally grateful for my husband who continues to be a great support to me and the family.

Anyone who is a mother will know that we constantly worry and find it hard to shut off. Men seem more able to even though they care the same. Mick has been a calming influence and is so very compassionate, but men seem to be more logical than women. They seem to be able to sleep even when times are so very stressful. Not me. The hours drag as I toss and turn, worry and fret, waiting for morning to come as a welcome relief.

As I lay in my bed one night, I could hear Paul sobbing and sounding as though he was in pain. I quickly woke Mick and together we went to his room where a sad sight awaited us.

Paul was shaking and losing control of his emotions. He was in great pain and cramping all over his body. He was sweating and having a panic attack and tremors. I felt such love and compassion, as I listened to his cry of pain pleading for us to help him. He was experiencing drug withdrawal symptoms.

There are those who have been in similar situations will understand the intense emotions felt at times like these. Although there are many compassionate people in the world who try to understand, only those who have experienced similar pain can truly know the anguish a mother feels when their child is crying out for help. There is such a feeling of helplessness.

While Mick tried to comfort him, I retired to my room and offered up a silent prayer of pleading. 'Please God help me, **IF ONLY** you can show me what I should do, as I cannot do this alone. Please, please help me.'

We could not stand by and watch and do nothing. We felt strongly that Paul needed medical assistance, and so we called the doctor as soon as morning came.

He had been our doctor for many years and was very aware of Paul's drug addiction. I felt confident he could help us in our hour of need.

When he arrived at our home, we explained what was happening and then left him alone with Paul. When the doctor joined us after seeing Paul, he shared his response with us. 'I have just told him to get up and clean his room.' No compassion, nothing. Paul had to go through withdrawal alone no help was forthcoming.

The days ahead were unbearable as we watched our son come out of the torment he was in. I was not expecting his reaction to be quite as harsh or uncaring as the doctor was also a Christian. I had no idea as what to do, or who to turn to apart from my husband, also suffering from the stress and strain of it all.

As always, Mick and I weathered the storm, but it was a tough time. Mick never wavered in his support and has always been a calming influence on me. I've also been blessed by his unconditional love. He's listened, encouraged and given me strength to carry on.

I will be forever grateful for him and the pure love of Christ he has for our family and all he has come into contact with. He is a true Christian, a wonderful husband and father. We have shared so much together, some things which I feel are far too personal to share outside of the family.

Many marriages have broken up because of the strain of dealing with a loved one on drugs. For many it becomes too difficult to deal with. Slowly love is replaced with anger, indifference, hopelessness, and then finally defeat.

The bad times would have been all-consuming and not only can the heart break but the spirit too. But Mick and I have sustained one another through the good and bad times which is what marriage is all about. Our faith has never wavered.

We would have many more tragic incidents to face in the future, and life would become almost unbearable.

Chapter XIV - Tough Love

"Reproving betimes with sharpness, when moved upon by the Holy Ghost; and then showing forth afterwards an increase of love toward him whom thou hast reproved, lest he esteem thee to be his enemy."

D&C 121:43

I was at breaking point and knew some tough decisions had to be made.

I explained to Paul that as much as I loved him, I was unable to support him in his current lifestyle. For the sake of everyone, I had no alternative but to ask him to find alternative accommodation and leave. I did, however, offer to help him find somewhere to live. Was that decision an answer to a prayer? **IF ONLY** I knew. I told him I loved him so much, but I was exhausted. I knew he would never be accepted back on to the council housing list again, but we needed our sanity back and had to consider the needs of our other children.

And so began the quest to find a flat which would be acceptable for Paul and his financial circumstances.

I didn't realise how difficult the task would be. Many hours, days and weeks were spent viewing what I can only describe as places unfit for habitation.

How some landlords can live with their conscience is beyond me. One such place was so small (one room) and in complete need of a makeover. It was filthy with paper coming off the walls and it had dirty worn furniture and a smell of urine. I felt like crying, not just for us, but for so many people who have to live in such awful conditions and are lining the pockets of unscrupulous landlords. It beggared belief that they could sleep in their beds knowing the situation of their tenants. Of course there were exceptions and some tenants abused the homes of their landlords, but there should be some guidelines before they rented to prospective tenants.

Hopefully that is not the case nowadays.

I have had many more instances since then of unscrupulous landlords and their lack of compassion for others. The condition of some of the accommodation did not reflect the prices they were charging either.

And so the search continued. Paul and I became very despondent. Hour after hour, day after day, week after week we searched through the local newspapers, trudged the streets hoping that relief would come soon.

Would we ever be able to find a suitable place to allow my son to have a roof over his head? I began to feel the guilt coming on again. Should I allow Paul to stay at home and make the best of a difficult situation? Should I watch as my son prepares to live in conditions that I as a mother should never allow?

I decided to keep on searching and praying for some relief soon. **IF ONLY** my prayers could be answered.

We existed from day-to-day not knowing what the new one would bring.

I had to face the world and carry on looking after the needs of my family - outwardly smiling but inwardly crying. No one will ever know the true extent of my suffering not even my family. I tried to hide from them the degree of my pain and sorrow.

Only those who have been through a similar trial because that is what it was, can possibly understand how helpless, alone and vulnerable one can feel at times like this.

All I could do was pray with all my heart and strength that some relief would come soon and allow us to have a return to some normality in our lives. How I prayed.

I have had to learn over the years that some prayers are answered immediately, some later, and some will not be answered until the next life. It takes great faith to accept the Lord's will and not our own.

During these difficult years, my parents visited with us from Cornwall on a regular basis and it seemed an ideal opportunity for us to have a family photograph taken while they were with us.

They were not aware of the full extent of our situation and how serious it was. We did our best to keep everything as normal as possible and try to enjoy our time together.

We were preparing to take the family photograph when the doorbell rang.

It was with a heavy heart that I faced the police on the doorstep. They enquired as to whether Paul was with us. When we replied, the officer announced that they had come to arrest him.

I felt numb with shock. I nervously asked if we could take one family photograph before he was taken away, as my parents were visiting with us from far away. The answer was negative, and the police insisted on immediately searching his room.

After what seemed like hours, but were only minutes, the police returned downstairs and told us no drugs had been found, but they were still arresting him for further questioning.

He was released the next day, and no further charges were made. What a relief it was to hear those words! But I also realised that although drugs had not been found, it did not mean he was not taking them or that our challenges were over.

But at least I could de-stress for a while, once again, and try to make the most of our time with my parents.

I still look back and wonder why we were not allowed one photograph while my family was together in the home. They could have ensured that Paul would not slip out, but they were adamant and so our family group photo including Paul never happened that night. Sadly, we did not have the opportunity to do another one in the future. We tried to smile, but the photograph did not reflect the way we were feeling.

My parents were understanding and were non-judgmental. They loved Paul so much and could not understand how he had become involved in such a way of life. They remembered what a wonderful baby and well-mannered boy he was.

We got through the time they were with us trying to act as normally as possible. We were determined that they enjoyed their stay with us and would return home with happy memories.

But it was a difficult nevertheless.

Following my parent's departure, we continued our search to find accommodation for Paul, and on turning up to view a particular flat was informed it had just gone. Fortunately, another one had just become available in the same block.

It was a two-bedroomed place and not for a single tenant,

but the landlord was willing to let Paul view it and if suitable, he would agree to him renting it.

The place left a lot to be desired. By this time we were desperate and decided this was about the best it was going to get.

I offered a silent prayer of thanks in my heart to know I could see my son settled once again, and we could hopefully sleep more soundly at night.

And so Paul once again settled into a new home, and I hoped he would see the error of his ways and try and turn his life around.

Each Sunday after Church either Mick or I would go to his home and pick him up for lunch. I would wonder what the other tenants were like and would they have a bad influence on him. One thing I learned over the years was that I could only help if help was accepted.

Family photograph (excluding Paul) with my parents

Chapter XV -
Hope Once Again

"Wherefore, if a man have faith he must needs have hope; for without faith there cannot be any hope."

Book of Mormon - Moroni 7:42

Paul refused any kind of help apart from meeting when it was convenient for him. He chose to live a private and secret life at other times. But he was slowly trying to put his life in order unbeknown to us, and I would learn years later to what extent he had succeeded.

He accepted an invitation to join us on a break to Scotland, and this would be the only special holiday he was blessed to have with us.

I had hoped and dreamed that one day we could all have one big family holiday together with all of our children and extended family. I pictured us in a sunny country staying in villas and swimming in our private pool! I imagined enjoying a wonderful family bonding time together as we laughed and played together.

IF ONLY our circumstances would have changed and my dream could have been a reality.

It would have been a once in a lifetime holiday. That would have been wonderful. **IF ONLY.**

Well it's good to dream sometimes. But sadly due to circumstances, the dream was never realised. We did manage to enjoy our holiday in Scotland, though. It was wonderful with the exception of the accommodation which was basically an old Nissan hut (tin shack)! Paul was the happiest we had seen him in a long time and he seemed to relish the whole experience, especially the beautiful scenery.

Paul on holiday with us in Scotland.

Mick and Paul during our holiday in Scotland.

We were aware, of course, that Paul was now on methadone, a drug developed to help those on heroin beat their addiction. He was also now being monitored on a regular basis, by Community and Drugs Counselling and he seemed to be coping with life so much better. But I was also aware that he would continue to fight and face the temptation that his addiction to drugs might return at any time. I knew this would be a challenge that he and I would probably have to face for the rest of his mortal life.

But oh the joy I felt as we savored every moment of our vacation time with him.

How he loved Scotland and I could see the joy he felt visiting so many wonderful places and sharing special times with us.

It's at times like these that one can feel closer to God and the wonders of the creation and what a wonderful world it is, spoilt only by some of mankind.

I was one happy Mum and my cup overflowed.

Following our holiday, Paul decided to join us for Christmas and visited with us on a more regular basis.

We had some very special times together. I could see him becoming more open and receptive as we talked one with another. I realised that the years we had tried with Paul had not been wasted.

Sometimes I would just sit and listen to Paul talk; it was wonderful. He had a great way with words and had such a lot of knowledge.

He loved his family so much and once remarked, 'If it wasn't for your love and support I would have ended my life by now.'

I am sure his faith had also played a part in recognising that taking one's life is not something that would be considered a wise decision.

During this time he continued to improve, and having acquired a motorbike from his biological father, he took a test and passed first time. Sadly, it amounted to nothing.

Sometime later it was announced that a new Temple was to be built in Preston. Following the completion and before the dedication, there would be an Open Day to allow members and visitors to walk around the grounds and view the interior of the Temple. I wasn't sure how Paul would react, but I decided to invite him to join us to attend an "Open Day" along with our son Simon and granddaughter Katherine, who having been baptised shortly before was very excited at the prospect.

I prayed he would join us and felt it might help him to be touched by the spirit and ponder on his life now and, how **IF ONLY** he would try and turn away from his addiction that he would have a future to look forward to.

It filled me with great joy when Paul accepted the invitation to join us. We made the trip specially and joined with others from our Ward later. Words cannot describe how happy I was to be with my son in the Temple of the Lord.

Preston, England Temple

It was a wonderful day, and I felt hope in my heart as we walked through those sacred rooms together. I could see by his countenance that he was feeling something special.

We didn't need to say a word, the spirit was enough to touch us both and we all felt a great love that day which will remain with me forever.

Life improved on a weekly basis. In August, the family enjoyed a wonderful time together when Mick and I celebrated our Silver Wedding anniversary at a nearby restaurant. Paul once again joined us and looked healthier and happier than I had seen him for a long time. He was trying so hard to turn his life around.

Celebrating our 25th wedding anniversary

In December I saw an advertisement in our local newspaper stating that our local Marina Centre was opening their doors for the first time to feed those who were in need on

Christmas day. Willing hands were needed.

This was a new venture in Great Yarmouth, but had been successfully running in Norwich. I felt it would be a way of helping others who needed love and understanding, and it would also help me to count my own blessings in my life.

Mick and I decided we would like to get involved. We found great joy in spending time with the people, listening to them as they shared with us the many varied situations they were in and the challenges they were facing. It was wonderful to see them enjoy a full Christmas dinner provided for them and witness a little joy and relief from their daily challenges.

This was also an opportunity for me to get Paul involved and for him to get something out of serving others.

I invited him to join with us, but he was very reluctant. Later I learned that for him mixing with the unemployed, struggling or addicted added to his depression. But he was more than happy for us to share in the Christmas spirit with others and meet with him later and celebrate together.

So many people from the Church also gave us support, especially the missionaries, and it was so uplifting to mingle with those who needed a little Christmas cheer.

It truly brought home to me the many varied and complex situations some had found themselves in, some not through any fault of their own and others through self-affliction. I felt great love for them and wished I could change their lives not only for just one day but forever.

I would often ponder as I watched these people what had been their situation for them to be at this point in their life?

I felt great love for them and saw them as children of God, who loves all people, and perhaps he felt at some of their sad situations.

I have always tried to look beyond the exterior of people and look into their hearts.

We all need to scatter a little sunshine wherever we go in life and bring joy and comfort to others. That is what our Savior spent his life doing and the following hymn "Scatter Sunshine" depicts that:

Scatter Sunshine

In a world where sorrow
Ever will be known,
Where are found the needy
And the sad and lone,
How much joy and comfort
You can all bestow,
If you scatter sunshine
Ev'rywhere you go.

(Chorus)
Scatter sunshine all along your way.
Cheer and bless and brighten
Ev'ry passing day.
Scatter sunshine all along your way.
Cheer and bless and brighten
Ev'ry passing day.

Slightest actions often
Meet the sorest needs,
For the world wants daily
Little kindly deeds.
Oh, what care and sorrow
You may help remove,
With your songs and courage,
Sympathy and love.
(Chorus)

When the days are gloomy,
Sing some happy song;
Meet the world's repining
With a courage strong.
Go with faith undaunted
Thru the ills of life;
Scatter smiles and sunshine
O'er its toil and strife.
(Chorus)

Text: Lanta Wilson Smith
Music: Edwin O. Excell, 1851-1921

Wonderful words which **IF ONLY** we all followed would unite us all in this very troubled world in which we live.

By January 1999, Paul again had no contact with us, and we knew this meant he had sunk into another depression.

This was another time of worrying, wondering and praying for my son who chose to separate himself from family and again wanted to be left alone to sort himself out.

There were so many years of broken promises and broken dreams.

When I feel there is a light at the end of a tunnel, too often, the light has been snuffed out, and darkness reigns again.

More long absences, more heartache and the pain of knowing within my heart that my son has succumbed to addiction again.

Not only does it affect me, but it has a ripple effect on all the family.

Those days seemed to drag even though I was busy as a mother. By this time I was holding down two part-time jobs as well as fulfilling my Church callings.

I found it hard to function and sleep did not come easily. I tossed and turned and imagined the unimaginable at times. **IF ONLY, IF ONLY, IF ONLY** would resound in my ears.

Sunday, the 20th of June was Father's Day, and Paul decided to pay us a visit. When I saw him he looked so unwell, and I asked him if he had been ill. He refrained from admitting if he had but said he did have some challenges. Apart from that I found it hard to get him to open up to me. He once again cut off contact with us with no explanation, preferring to be left alone, and we had to respect his wishes. Inwardly I worried and hoped he would be safe and able to cope.

In December Paul joined with us for Christmas and appeared relatively well. He was eating better and joined in the spirit of Christmas. He seemed to enjoy being with his family once again. And so began another period of regular visits with Paul eating with us every Sunday. Once again I would attend Church and then leave to pick him up for lunch. I felt so relieved to know that at least he was eating something substantial on a regular basis.

I saw a light at the end of the tunnel once again.

Over the years I have spent many days in fasting and prayer for my son, my prodigal son. At times it was hard to see that no matter how hard I prayed or fasted, it seemed to no avail. But I also came to realise that no matter how hard I tried, I in reality could do nothing. My son had his agency and was free to make choices for himself, but he would also have to face the consequences of his actions.

But I knew it was important for me to continue to plead for him and never give up. I needed to be the best example as I could and leave the rest to Paul.

During those years I received from Paul some lovely cards. He wrote eloquently declaring his love, respect and appreciation. He thanked me for standing by him in the bad times, not condoning what he had done, but giving him unconditional love as only a mother can.

He had a way with words and was far more intelligent than he was given credit for. I will never forget those wonderful words he wrote to me but prefer to keep them private. They brought me comfort in the knowledge that Paul loved me so much.

He truly loved all his family, and in his heart, I know he wanted what we had. But he said there were times when he didn't want to live. He couldn't see that light at the end of the tunnel.

Over the years I never heard him raise his voice to me. He was always respectful. And never swore or used profanity.

Paul, unlike some I have read about, never induced feelings of guilt in us. He had great love and respect for us, and years later he said that is why he distanced himself, to save us the heartache. This was his way. He never blamed or accused us of failing him in any way.

The parable "Prodigal Son" has great meaning to me, the story has touched my heart so many times and just like the father in the parable, he never gave up hope of his son returning. I knew that I would never give up either on my son returning to his family. But like the father, I too had to let my son go and hope one day he would return.

I could never be truly happy until things changed to a greater extent.

I prayed that my immediate family would understand that Paul needed me, and unlike the brother of the Prodigal son who resented the love his father had for him when he had been the faithful one, they would never feel resentment but unconditional love.

Thankfully they always supported me and loved Paul.

I do however remember one day my brother seeing me in

distress remarked, 'You are making yourself ill let him get on with it.'

There was no compassion shown towards Paul but I realised he didn't fully understand the depth of love of a mother. He was naturally concerned for me, and could see the effect it was having on me. I could only forgive and hope with time my brother would see the grief and pain I had and show me the love that I so badly needed. I was to see that love come to fruition many years later when my brother's heart was truly softened.

Prayer became my strength, not that the turmoil was taken away, but the ability to withstand and keep strong even when there were times I didn't want to. I must say that there were times when I did feel alone and at other times I felt as though my Savior was right by my side.

The poem "Footprints" became very meaningful and strengthened me during difficult times. It tells of a man who has a dream when he is walking along the beach with the Lord. He sees scenes from his life flashing before his eyes, and most of the time he sees two sets of footprints, his and the Lord's but during the lowest periods of his life there are only one set of footprints.

He questioned the Lord and asked Him, 'Why did you leave me when I needed you most?'

The answer came clear and unmistakable: 'When you see one set of footprints that is when I carried you.'

Over the years I to have spent many hours at sunrise walking along the beach. This has been my time to talk to the Lord and to feel His presence and express my love, thanks and concerns. I haven't needed footprints to prove He was there because I knew He was, but I also knew that I had to do my part and show my faith and then He has carried and strengthened me and enabled me to carry on. He still does and I find comfort and solace as I spend my "private" moments alone with Him on our beach.

Chapter XVI - Farewell Son

"And may the Lord bless your soul, and receive you at the last day into his
kingdom, to sit down in peace. Now go, my son, and teach the word unto
this people. Be sober. My son, farewell."

Book of Mormon - Alma 38:15

In 2000 our youngest son Simon was called to serve a mission
in Cape Town for two years.

His initial training for his mission would be at the Preston
Mission Training Centre, adjacent to the Preston Temple, and
was to report there on the 27th December.

Simon had been courting a young lady for some time
and had got engaged to her. We knew this would make the
parting more difficult for both of them, but it was what they
both wanted. Simon's girlfriend asked us if she could move
from her parent's home at Wisbech, Norfolk and come and
live with us while Simon was away on his mission, and we
happily agreed.

On the 26th of December, Simon was set apart as a
missionary by the Stake President. Simon had asked Paul to
attend with other members of the family and also to travel with
us to the Preston Missionary Training Centre (MTC) where
we would say our goodbyes.

He had a very special bond with his brother, but Paul
could not bring himself to go, although he did attend
Simon's farewell party. As usual, he found it difficult with
so many people there, and I am sure he was relieved when
it was over.

He withdrew into himself finding it all too much. Knowing
it would be two years before he would see Simon again made
it very difficult to say a personal goodbye. Over the years they
had built up such a very close relationship, and they had spent

many hours together watching football and talking into the early hours of the morning.

Paul did spend Christmas with us though. We all tried to appear outwardly happy, but knowing Simon was leaving two days later made it difficult.

We left very early the morning of the 27th following Simon's setting apart after a very happy but emotional evening. We made our journey to Preston and said our goodbyes to our son at the Mission Training Centre. Here he would spend the next few weeks before he left to serve his mission in Africa. As all mothers will know and understand, there is a mixture of sadness, pain, joy and extreme pride to witness another son leaving his family to serve the Lord in other lands.

Paul seemed subdued and quiet in the following days, and I know he was not only missing his brother but was feeling guilty at not saying goodbye. But he made up for this by writing some lovely letters to him and putting his feelings into words.

Once again we had a routine and Paul would come over each Sunday and join us for lunch.

During these visits, we took the opportunity to talk with him and shared many wonderful memories of his childhood years and the great bond we had as a family with his brothers and sisters.

Paul always showed interest in our morning at Church. He would want to know what the theme of the service was and who the speakers were. Not once did I hear Paul deny the Church or speak irreverently about it, in fact quite the reverse.

I know he respected us and the way we lived. I also know in my heart that Paul would have had many times when he reflected on his decision to leave the Church and no doubt regretted the path he had taken.

He regularly attended counselling sessions and was tested for drugs each time, but he had never been offered a test for hepatitis. Considering Paul had been on drugs, and in the past had been sharing needles, surely this test should have been a priority? Years later his sister had advised Paul to request that these be carried out, and Paul admitted that he had been reluctant to do so before because he was scared to know what the results might be.

Some of the symptoms he had been experiencing were similar to those of his friends, and he was naturally worried.

She explained as gently as she could that whatever the outcome, it was still important to get the tests done and to know the results good or bad as delaying them could have a detrimental effect on his health.

In the meantime methadone was regularly prescribed and he was encouraged to reduce the dose from time to time. Sometimes he coped well, but at other times the medicine needed to be increased depending on his mental state. But from a substance point of view, Paul was doing very well.

In 2001 we took him to Worcester to visit Mick's family, and it was so good to see the change in him and the effort he was making to bond with us again.

He so loved the Malvern Hills and would sit and contemplate the stunning views from the top.

I am sure it was a time of pondering, too. In and around the area of the Malvern Hills, great missionary work was accomplished. A wonderful place to feel the spirit and reflect on the important part this area played in the gospel. We had a wonderful few days and but our joy was short lived when Paul received a phone call from a friend informing him that his flat had been broken into.

He became very agitated and shaky, and we knew we would have to return home and find out the extent of the burglary. This set Paul back again, and he slipped into depression once more.

On returning home we entered the flat to find he had indeed been burgled, but the intruder had been disturbed and very little had been taken. Sadly, some money had gone and some other items which Paul needed and I felt so sorry for him.

Having been burgled twice I knew the effect this can have on someone, and this burglary was probably carried out by someone who knew Paul.

To make matters worse, life began to become intolerable living where he was. He had a new landlord and new problems with many very undesirable tenants moving in. No maintenance was carried out and the flat was by now in a bad state of repair.

Paul was desperate to move as he was trying to turn his life around, and he struggled to fit in with those around him.

Once again our life was thrown into chaos and confusion, but somehow we managed to survive each crisis and be strengthened by our faith and our determination to "never give up". But there were times when it became an almost impossible task.

During these traumatic years we still had to confront other challenges that beset us and tried our patience and faith to the very limit.

In July 2001 I underwent a major operation and Paul was there for me and showing so much empathy and caring that it touched my heart. Unfortunately Mick was away in Denmark at the time I was requested to check into the hospital, but I was grateful for all my children and their families who gave me the support I needed and helped in my recovery. Over the years I had been there for Paul, and now had been there for me.

These are times which stay in my memory. Throughout the bad spells I always knew that Paul loved his family and wished he had made better choices in his life. I am also sure that is the case for so many others who have wandered off the path and found themselves unable to break away from the situation they have got themselves in.

Paul had continually expressed his desire to change, and he tried many times, but each time he failed to accomplish what he had set out to do and would constantly say

'**IF ONLY** I had a computer. **IF ONLY** I had the money. **IF ONLY** I felt well. **IF ONLY** I had transport.'

I too have used that phrase so many times in my life **IF ONLY** we hadn't moved. **IF ONLY** I had known. **IF ONLY** I had done this. **IF ONLY** I hadn't got divorced. **IF ONLY, IF ONLY, IF ONLY.**

Life is full of **IF ONLY** so it seems.

During this time my mother's health was beginning to deteriorate, and she had become a danger to herself. On one occasion while my father had left her for a short while in the bathroom, he returned and discovered her attempting to climb into the bath of very hot water. My father had to quickly remove her from a dangerous situation.

She would switch on the electric kettle without first filling it with water. She had become very confused and frail.

Sometime later she was admitted to hospital due to dehydration and became very forgetful. She became ill and fell out of bed several times injuring herself in the process.

Poor Dad was at wit's end.

Mick and I decided to travel down to visit her and were saddened to see her condition. This wasn't the Mum I knew.

She looked so small and vulnerable that I found it difficult to sit by her bedside and watch her as she pleaded to go home.

We did what we could to try and help alleviate the pain of Mum and Dad. We helped as much as possible, physically and emotionally, and as our time with them came to an end, we said a sad farewell, returning home with heavy hearts.

Chapter XVII -
Another Guilt Trip

"One day your life will flash before your
eyes so make sure it's worth watching"

Unknown Author

My lovely mother was eventually diagnosed with Alzheimer's disease. So, we travelled to Cornwall to visit with her again and assist the family in looking for a suitable nursing home.

My Dad found it hard to accept. He was very distressed at the thought of his wife of seventy years no longer able to communicate and relate to him and the family.

To add to our stress, my brother was taken ill and urgently needed a triple heart bypass. This meant he was unable to look after Mum and Dad while he was recuperating.

These were very difficult times.

Mick and I soon found it necessary to travel extensively from Norfolk to Cornwall, as my mother's situation worsened. Sadly, my father, who was also struggling with the stress of it all, eventually had to go into a home apart from Mum.

Dad moved into a residential home because he was of sound mind, but physically unable to cope. Mum was put into a nursing home where she would receive the full-care she needed. Because they had different circumstances, it was not possible for them to be together. The world seemed so unfair.

I suggested Dad move in with us back in Great Yarmouth, but he declined not wanting to be too far from Mum. We did our utmost to travel and be with them as often as time permitted, but being a sixteen hour round-trip, it was not an easy task and Mick of course had work commitments.

Dad would constantly ring me and cry saying "he could not

cope" and pleaded saying "I can't take any more please help me" but he still refused to live with us. By now, he had chosen not to visit Mum anymore because he found her condition so difficult.

I must add that by this time Dad had moved care homes about four different times. Each time stating he was not happy where he was. Even in his last home, he failed to settle and remained in his room refusing to mix with the other residents. In all fairness to him, the majority of residents were female and there were only two males. Looking back, I do feel he could have been treated with more kindness and respect.

The home he was in left a lot to be desired, but that's another story.

Dad retained his faculties to the end and was very much aware of how he was treated.

When we were in Plymouth, I did meet with those who were responsible for my Dad's care and shared my concerns but living so far away made it very difficult to be more diligent than I was.

IF ONLY I had lived closer I might have been more helpful, but I will be forever grateful for my two brothers and their families, who did the very best they could. It must have been extremely difficult as by this time my sister-in-law had been diagnosed with terminal cancer. This necessitated my brother, the one who had the heart bypass, to care for his wife.

My Dad continued to plead for help, and I felt very guilty as I listened on the telephone so far away to his pleas and tears of distress.

All I could do was to offer him a home here with us which he constantly refused.

As another alternative, I suggested we move Mum to a nursing home in Great Yarmouth and Dad could come and live with us. He wasn't happy with that idea and continued to phone and relate how unhappy he was and how hard it was for him.

IF ONLY he would have listened to me, but his mind was made up.

The phone calls became a regular occurrence with Dad in distress on one end and me on the other continually offering to have him live with us. He wouldn't listen and there wasn't another solution for him.

We were at a loss as to what else could be done for him. It was an impossible situation.

I continually went on my guilt trips, but knew there was little I could do apart from listen and comfort myself that he did have other family members close by who did their utmost to help and support him. But being the only daughter, I suppose Dad felt he could relate to me more.

He had very little idea of the stress we were under, and I chose to keep it from him so as not to worry him further. If I am honest, I did have fear of the reaction I would receive had he known the full truth of our sad situation here.

If he had known the full extent of our challenges with Paul, I know it would have made our life so much more difficult. And so I continued to withhold much from Dad giving him a little information but never enough to change my relationship with him.

But these many challenges would stand my husband in good stead in the years ahead when he was Bishop once again. Having experienced pain and sorrow himself, he could relate to others with challenges in their lives and feel their grief and empathize with love and understanding it has helped me too; although I consider myself to be a compassionate person and have empathy for others, it became more vivid to me in the years ahead.

It seems to me that no experience is ever wasted. We do find strength in adversity and I have seen the strength in other members of our family who have overcome challenges and been stronger for it.

But would we have chosen the challenges? I'm not sure. Sometimes it can take years before we see the "whys" but eventually it does become clear to us.

But it takes great strength and fortitude to weather the storms of life without a murmur, and there were times that I did murmur! But I take comfort in the knowledge that even the Prophet Lehi's wife Sariah in The Book of Mormon murmured when times were difficult.

We are all imperfect beings here on the earth and striving to overcome the natural man in us, and we will be forever striving to better ourselves.

When I was called as Relief Society President, I felt very

overwhelmed with the challenges I was to face, but I felt at peace during and following my being "set apart". I was promised I would be able to fulfill my calling with the support of my husband. I would be an example to the sisters and be able lift them up. I would help them to grow and that I would be blessed with health and strength to my body.

I saw the fulfillment of that blessing and had such wonderful support from my counselors that enabled me to serve the sisters in the Church diligently. I hope they felt the same.

In October we held a special "Make a difference Day", and with help from Ward members, we managed to make 25 quilts for those in deprived parts of the world.

Jumping ahead to 2007, Mick and I were very fortunate to visit the LDS Welfare Square in Salt Lake City. I remember the emotions I felt when I saw, amongst many other things, so many quilts donated by sisters from the Relief Society ready for dispatch to those in need. I felt such joy that we were able to play a small part in reaching out to others.

I remember watching a film depicting the welfare work that Church members were involved in and feeling the spirit very strongly. As we were leaving, two wonderful sister missionaries sang "Because I have been Given Much". It was so emotionally beautiful.

Clothes donated to the Church at
Welfare Square for the needy

In 2002 we managed to rent another flat for Paul, much to our relief, and arranged for him to move to his new home. He was trying so hard to turn his life around but the environment he was currently in was not helping him in his endeavor. He was now living an almost reclusive life. He had cut himself off from those he knew who were involved in drugs, but all around him was temptation, and it was imperative we helped him move to a place of safety.

His new accommodation was one of the best we had seen thus far.

I was so relieved. It was clean and nicely decorated and had a kitchen with sitting room, bathroom and bedroom. I helped to settle Paul in. Mick was away at the time and I felt a sense of relief that at last our son was living in a clean and pleasant home and in a much more select area to his former place.

He settled in well and became more united with the family once again.

This was the best we had seen Paul. He regularly attended a clinic for help with his methadone addiction and received counseling on a regular basis. This was not an ideal situation, of course, but we put our trust in those who deal with these situations daily, and hope with time and support, Paul would be able to wean off drugs altogether.

He joined a pool team at a local pub and seemed to be so much happier making friends with those not involved in the drugs scene. Having this new social life helped to get him out into the community and give him a new lease of life.

But one night while playing in a match game with his team, there was an incident and Paul was attacked with a cue. The result was Paul being taken to the hospital for stitches. The reason for it I believe was the attacker had been drinking and lost control. Later, having sobered up, he expressed his remorse for what he had done.

Paul was also in a darts team and it was a step forward in the right direction, as it was also helping him to become part of "normal" society.

During these years I had to learn to be patient and hope with time, support and love that I would one day see my son stay on the right path and live the gospel once more. I had gained such a strong testimony over the years and I lived it with all of my heart to the best of my ability.

I was concerned as to Paul's eternal destiny and often wondered what would happen if he did not turn his life around fully.

The scripture in Alma 42:32 from The Book of Mormon was shared so many times in our various Church classes that it became embedded in my mind and caused me to worry continually as to Paul's eternal welfare.

"For behold this is the time for men to prepare to meet God; yea, behold the day of this life is the day for men to prepare to perform their labors".

I loved Paul so much, and the thought of being separated from him in the eternities was unthinkable. I cannot think of any mother who could imagine life without her loved ones and never having the opportunity to be reunited with them when we have passed from this life.

Over time Paul made many friends, male and female, and I could see the impact this was having on him and his self-esteem. He had become an avid follower of Manchester United football team, and I believe never missed a football match on TV when they were playing. He was also able to see a live game with some family members in Manchester.

Simon, our youngest who supported Newcastle United, spent many hours watching Match of the Day with Paul when family members were in bed. They would talk about their teams and players and how they performed. There was always a rivalry when their teams would play against each other, but Manchester would always win apart from one match when Newcastle beat Manchester 5-0.

Simon would always remind him of that win, but Paul would smile and just say it was a fluke.

Simon said Paul would drive him crazy at times with his obsession over the TV remote control and would constantly go through all the programmes repeatedly checking the TV guide.

I witnessed a change of heart in Paul that warmed my spirit and at last I could see a difference.

Over the years I had begun to feel a hostage in some ways.

I felt I could never be really happy again until Paul had put his life in order. As someone once related to me, "it is like walking on a minefield, every time we try to make a difference our best efforts can blow up in front of us often making the addiction worse, it can be a risky business".

Now I felt as though I was being released as a hostage, and I felt freer than I had for many years.

I have learned there is no single right answer or clear road map for those members of families of the addicted. What is right for one is not necessarily right for another. Different strategies work for different people.

I can recall many well-meaning people who seem to think they have the solution to everything. I have had to turn the cheek many times and literally bite my tongue as they gave their opinions and counsel me on what I should do. Although they meant well, they never had to experience a portion of the pain my family and I had suffered.

During one particular occasion when I was visiting with a family member, he noted the distress in my voice as I shared my feelings with him and recounted some of the difficulties I had. I was hoping for some comfort from him to lift my spirits, but instead he told me in words, not to be repeated, to wash my hands of him. I fled in tears as I had not expected that response. There were many more occasions when words spoken thoughtlessly could have killed me emotionally, but I learned that that which does not kill us makes us stronger.

I am who I am today. I am a strong woman because of my experiences, however painful they have been. They have molded me and helped me to more fully understand others and to be more Christ-like and less judgmental.

We are told life is a journey and we cannot go around it - we have to go through it. And what a journey it is! For some, it seems easier than for others. We cannot always understand the reasons for this, but the world is full of people who have had to overcome some of the most traumatic and devastating experiences that we cannot always comprehend and they question, "Why me"?

Words fail me sometimes as to the answers to this question.

Some trials are self-inflicted, but others come to good and faithful people for reasons we may not understand until we leave this life.

I would certainly not want to compare myself to the Prophet Joseph Smith, but I often think of him and his family and the unrelenting pressure and trials and persecution that they had to endure until his death. This gave me strength to keep on going when the going got tough.

Here was a man who had received a vision and was chosen to restore the gospel to the earth once again.

This was no ordinary man.

Joseph had to have complete faith in the Lord to endure the many trials that would be his lot in life and be willing to submit his will to the Lord knowing that all would be well if he was patient. At the age of thirty-eight, he would lose his life at the hands of others. However, he was prepared. He knew that death was not the end, and he would receive an eternal reward for remaining faithful.

Because of him I have the gospel in my life and have learned so much about the Plan of Salvation. Where I came from, why I am here, and where I can go when this earthly life is over if I stay true to my faith.

That is why every time I reached a point where I couldn't take any more, I did. I came to realise that we are so much stronger than we give ourselves credit for.

My trials are insignificant in comparison to some, and I know that if I keep the faith and do the best I can, I will be given the strength to overcome no matter what the outcome may be in this life.

I need to keep focused and grounded and have the faith to trust in God, as he is aware of my pain and the desires of my heart.

On the 6th of December 2003 at 3:30am, I received a phone call from my brother informing me that my Mum had passed away. Although sad, it was a happy release from her sad existence of living in a nursing home and separated from loved ones.

We had made many visits to see her, and each time it became more difficult to witness, wanting to cry at the injustice of it all.

She had been a wonderful mother and her life had been difficult. Her ending was not one I would have wished for. She had had numerous falls and had suffered to the end.

Although this story is not about my mother, some of the events played a part in the added stress I was going through. It was so hard to witness the conditions that not only my mother had to live through but also the other residents where she was too. People were at different stages with their illness, and I remember one dear lady who in an advanced stage of Alzheimer's had become aggressive and attacked my mother.

It was at times like this that I wanted to rescue her and have her live with me, but she needed 24hr care by this time which could only be given by those who were responsible for her in the care home.

But it didn't take away the pain that a daughter feels for her mother. I still have the memories of a mother who was so caring, funny, and compassionate and had always been there for me.

She had been a full-time mother and her whole life was dedicated to her children. Our Dad had spent a large portion of his time serving in the Royal navy and separated from us for long absences, usually two years at a time.

And so it was with a mixture of sadness and relief that I received the news that Mum had passed away. How I wished I could have been with her in her final hours.

Mick was away at sea and I arose early from my bed feeling

too restless to sleep with so many thoughts and emotions going through my mind.

No one to talk to and many hours before my family would be awake. I refrained from waking them and their children until a more respectable hour knowing they could do very little to help apart from listen and comfort.

It was a Sunday morning, and I decided to carry on as usual in my calling as Relief Society President knowing that my Mum was at peace. I would feel the comfort spiritually and cope with the knowledge that I had of the eternal plan of Heavenly Father and that Mum was with those she loved.

What better place could I be than in God's house feeling the spiritual comfort needed at a time like this.

Following the sacrament service I regularly picked Paul up for lunch, and he was visibly moved when I told him his grandmother had passed away. He decided to attend the funeral with other members of family, and I was very touched and moved at his desire to pay his last respects to her.

He truly loved his grandmother, and this being his first experience of a close family death, he was shaken. She was a wonderful person, full of love for others and a desire to help those less fortunate.

Having been blessed with good health for a large part of her life and appearing younger than her years, my mother had constantly helped her friends and neighbors who needed assistance with shopping and bathing - even though they were sometimes so much younger than her!

She had great love for her children and grandchildren and indeed all she came into contact with. Was it any wonder Paul loved her and wanted to pay his last respects?

This may seem unimportant to my story, but to me it was another step in the right direction for Paul.

Here was Paul outwardly showing that he loved his family when for years he had distanced himself from those he loved rather than get emotionally involved. Not that he cared less; it was just the way he dealt with his emotions at the time.

The road ahead was a mixture of joy and pain.

Things were going in a positive direction and I felt a surge of relief at the visible change that I saw in Paul. He was determined to make something of his life and decided to do a computer course. I thought it would be a good idea if I joined him and give him support that would help him get his confidence back.

But it wasn't long before his confidence took a tumble again when he learned that a former friend of his had been found dead from a heroin overdose.

Like Paul, he had been an addict and had made many efforts to change his life, but each time his addiction had won until he was persuaded to take a college course.

He came off drugs, successfully completed a welding course and acquired employment with a reputable offshore company, but sadly this came to an end when he was made redundant sometime later. It wasn't long after this that he turned back to drugs and sadly died from the effects of heroin overdose.

Paul and I attended the funeral out of respect. It saddened me to witness the grief of his parents who were very respectable people and too lovely to be burdened with such a tragedy.

Paul found the period of time disturbing, and once again withdrew into himself asking for space to grieve, which was understandable.

But for me, it was another setback just when things seemed to be improving and life seemed to be more tolerable. As a mother I struggled to come to terms with the futility of it all. My heart went out to their families and the anguish they were suffering.

Sadly this would not be the last death. We would hear of others who Paul had known and sadly lost their lives because of addiction.

Night after night, I would lay awake and mourn for those who had lost their loved ones and at such a young age. Most of them came from good homes and knowing this made the reality of it so much more difficult.

Why did they throw it all away? For most, it seemed the problems started in their teens and they did not have the courage to resist the temptation of drugs or see the effects these drugs were having on their friends.

As members of the Church, we knew the reality of the adversary. We knew how they often use power to influence us if we so allow them, to drag us down but sometimes so gently we are not aware until they have us in their grasp.

I wish I could convince others of the danger of making very bad choices. I have tried many times to do so, but I am unable to reach the many who live for today and think "tomorrow we die" and that is it. So they make the most of it so to speak. **IF ONLY** they understood The Plan of Salvation.

We live in difficult times, but many would argue it has always been this way. This is true up to a point, but it has escalated extensively over the years. With progress comes opposition in all things. It can be used for the good of man or to their downfall. The choice is ours. But with the choices come consequences.

It is only by living the gospel, reading, praying and listening to a living Prophet and those who serve with him that we can understand more fully and have a clearer view. This includes: where we came from, why we are here and the eternal blessings that can be ours if we choose the right in this mortal life.

It wasn't long before we faced another challenge. Our eldest daughter separated from her husband, and once again, I grieved as only a mother can.

I will not dwell on the circumstances, but we were to face many years of unbearable sadness and pain until the divorce was finalised. It was heartrending to see the suffering of the whole family and witness the pain that divorce does to the human heart.

By this time Paul was in regular contact with us, and many hours were spent discussing every issue that affected us all whether it was illness, death, religion, politics and life in general. Whatever it was, Paul seemed to think he had the solution to everything. Or so he thought. He was very intelligent and amazed me with his knowledge.

But I still mourned for the son who I once had and was now a very different person physically. He looked so ill at times and was so lethargic, constantly falling asleep and struggling to walk. His skin was pallid, and he took to wearing some basic makeup to disguise his condition but to no avail.

He attended his support clinic on a regular basis and was

monitored as to his physical condition and mental state, but he resented the fact that so often his support workers would change. He would then have to relate to the new person from the beginning his past. This would only bring back memories that were best forgotten and he was trying to move on with his life.

In October my brother's wife passed away after much suffering, and it seemed that as soon as we overcame one hurdle we had to face another one.

There was yet another funeral for us to attend and more sadness at her passing.

Paul became depressed once again and found everything too much. Bad news seemed to affect him badly, and I often wondered if he viewed his own mortality at times like this.

He had days when he preferred to be left alone, and at times like these, there was little contact, which was very disconcerting and worrying. I had no idea how he was coping. But this was the way he chose to live, and we had to respect his wishes.

On February 14, 2004 our youngest son Simon, having returned from his mission in South Africa married his girlfriend, but Paul decided not to attend the wedding still suffering depression. I am sure he felt a mixture of sadness and happiness. He was happy for his brother but sad that he would not be around so often to spend time with him.

Chapter XVIII –
The Joy of Service

"When ye are in the service of your fellow beings
ye are only in the service of your God."

Book of Mormon - Mosiah 2:17

In March I prepared for our Relief Society Social, and many hours were put in to ensure our sisters had a wonderful evening. The theme was based on the Philippines and how the sisters who lived there served in the Church and community.

It was a wonderful night and very well attended. It was also an opportunity for us all to put our challenges to one side and enjoy the moment.

I suppose looking back I had always managed to keep busy especially when I was a Relief Society President. There were others who needed my support and caring too.

We had so much fun at our lovely Relief Society Socials where we learned about different countries and their traditions, cultures, food etc. Some of the countries our themes were based on over the years were: Italy, Greece, Cyprus, America and the Philippines. I remember when we had our American evening; a friend of ours who was very good at   impersonating Elvis Presley agreed to be our secret guest. He was so entertaining! The friendship grew and we visited him and his family on regular occasions.

In the near future we would see them going through a very difficult time which I will share with you later in my story. The Relief Society Socials were an annual event we looked forward to. We built some wonderful memories and the sisters were united and very supportive. We of, course, did not detract from the true purpose of the evening and shared with our sisters the way others were serving in Relief Society in various parts of the world.

Easter bonnet parade for Relief Society.
My daughter Karen is just behind me.

A fun evening. I am the chimney sweep.

A school skit with some of my family. Mick is the headmaster.

*Frosty the Snowman with Julie and two of
our Grandchildren. Mick is Frosty.*

Mick and me at a Western evening.

Primary.

Primary activity. A circus theme.

I took part in speech and musical festivals, variety shows and roadshows and I have wonderful memories of those special times. They were great fun and helped me to keep my mind occupied.

And of course there were: Visiting Teaching workshops to organise, compassionate service to tend to, Visiting Teaching, lessons, and meetings to attend. Life was hectic, but that was good because it helped me to forget my own challenges **IF ONLY** for a short while.

During this time I kept feeling very strongly that Mick, who had previously been a Bishop, was going to be recalled. The feeling wouldn't leave me, but I refrained from sharing it with my husband, who unbeknown to me, was also having the same feelings.

In June 2004 a social evening was held to say goodbye to a mature couple who were leaving to serve a mission in Beirut. At the conclusion of the evening, I was given some leftover food to take home, and as Mick was away, I decided to give it to a family member. It was very dark and late as I drove to their house and turning a corner, I noticed some children playing with a football on the pavement.

They were aware of me and I of them, and they stood on the pavement as their ball went into the road, waiting for me to drive past. As I slowly drove towards them, the ball went towards the car and a young lad of eight decided to make a dash for it. The next thing I heard was a thud and glass breaking. *I had hit the boy.*

What happened next seemed unreal. The police and ambulance arrived on the scene very quickly, and I was tested to see if I had been drink-driving. I was treated with great understanding, and they assured me I was not to blame, but unless someone has experienced it for themselves, it is hard to put into words the shock of it all.

I spent that night unable to sleep and felt very alone as Mick was away on business. I refrained from phoning and telling him knowing he could not really help me.

The next day he arrived home. I poured my heart out to him and he was very understanding and comforting. During the day we received a phone call from our Stake President asking to see us before Church began the next morning.

He extended to Mick the calling of Bishop of the Gorleston Ward once again. I remember sitting and crying, and the Stake President turning to me and asking me if I was upset that Mick was being called. I assured him I was not. I then explained I was still in shock from having knocked a little boy over, and that was the reason for my tears.

Later Mick shared with me he knew by the spirit he was to be called as Bishop again and was prepared. And so was I.

It was such a relief when the police informed me that the boy I had hit was recovering at home, and we were able to visit with him and the family. I was very apprehensive wondering what their reaction would be, but they were very understanding much to my relief.

During October I was released as Relief Society President and felt great sadness as I had so enjoyed my time serving the sisters.

Paul was on a regular dose of methadone during this period and being monitored weekly for any other substances present in his body. The tests were satisfactory and apart from the approved drug, he was free from illicit substances. This was wonderful news and a step in the right direction.

I was soon extended another calling again, this time as a Sunday school teacher to those investigating the Church, and I grew to love doing this. Working within the missionary programme helped to strengthen one's testimony, and I truly felt the spirit as I taught investigators and new members over the next two years.

My biggest challenge was dealing with Paul's mental and physical health, and it was a constant battle trying to be a good wife and mother, fulfill my callings in the Church and be there for my son.

I began to wonder whether our life would ever be normal again, and I had days when I felt isolated, sad, helpless and at a loss. But soon Christmas was approaching and my spirits lifted again. No time to sit and worry. Christmas was a happy occasion and Paul joined us for two days seeming happy and glad to be with us.

On Boxing Day we would have a large family gathering with around eighteen of us enjoying fun and games, and our son-in-law Kenny delighted in sharing with us his magical talents.

Each year I, like many others, wondered what the New Year would bring and I would quietly wish for the same things, peace in the world, good health, and some private and personal prayers answered.

By this time Paul was slowly deteriorating. There were constant trips to hospital, numerous blood tests and much concern as to his overall health.

There were days when he was unable to get out of bed and attend his appointments.

It was always difficult to sit and wait while he had yet another lot of blood tests. They could only take the blood from his feet, as the veins in his arms had collapsed from years of drug abuse when he was injecting intravenously.

I always kept outwardly composed for his sake but inside I was in turmoil.

There were good days and bad days, but to see my son slowly changing and witness the mental and physical suffering was very hard to bear.

In April 2005, my Dad passed away which for us and him was a happy release but nevertheless a very sad time. The days spent in a home were very unhappy for him. He had spent long, lonely hours in his room waiting to die.

This meant yet another funeral, another journey, and another talk for Mick to give. It also meant another relapse for Paul who once again chose to isolate himself from family.

In June 2005 I was called as a counselor in the Young

Women. This was a shock. I had this feeling that maybe I was too old and the young women would not accept me. But I gave my best effort, loved them and served them with as much enthusiasm as I could muster. I do believe they loved and appreciated me. I hope so.

While we were attending my father's funeral, our youngest son had moved back into our home having separated from his wife after a very difficult time.

Paul had always had a very close relationship with his brother, and he was very upset at the sadness of the situation. Over the weeks and months ahead, they would be a great support and comfort to each other leading up to Simon's divorce.

Simon would later marry a young lady from Missouri and settle in St. George, Utah.

Paul found it difficult to say goodbye once again because of the many hours they had spent together. But, of course, he was happy for him too.

As I look back in life, I often reflect on how my faith has seen me through everything. I wish all of my family were members of the Church and would know the strength it would have given them too.

My faith means everything to me, and I am so thankful to have found the truth and the help it has given me over the years.

I remember a sister once reading out a statement in Relief Society during a lesson based on Jesus Christ. She handed out a picture of the Savior with the words, "I didn't say it would be easy I only said it would be worth it". I have kept that picture and those words in my heart to this day.

In October 2005 Paul received a letter informing him that his incapacity allowance was to be stopped, and it would be replaced with Jobseeker's Allowance.

He became very agitated and felt he would not be able to cope if the payment was withdrawn.

For quite some time, he was unable to function properly and found everything a struggle. There were days when he was unable to walk, and he was constantly tired, bloated and ill. The timing could not have been worse.

I had seen Paul gradually deteriorating, lacking energy and putting on weight although he was eating less. There were days when he found it difficult to cope mentally and physically. To withdraw his incapacity allowance now was detrimental to his whole wellbeing.

His support worker decided to write a letter and confirm that Paul was not fit to work. She asked them to reconsider their decision. **IF ONLY** they had listened. But their decision was final, and within a short space of time, his money was stopped. He was told he would need to appeal if he felt the verdict was not justified.

In the meantime, it became necessary for us to support him financially and to see to his needs. The last thing we needed was for Paul to lose his home and again see him spiral out of control and undo all the good that had been done so far.

There was still a long way to go for Paul, but I had to be thankful for any progress that had been made and there certainly had been.

There is always something to be grateful for, no matter what our challenges may be. That is the reason why I love the following hymn:

Count Your Blessings

When upon life's billows you are tempest-tossed,
When you are discouraged, thinking all is lost,
Count your many blessings; name them one by one,
And it will surprise you what the Lord has done.
(Chorus)

Count your blessings;
Name them one by one.
Count your blessings;
See what God hath done.
Count your blessings;
Name them one by one.
Count your many blessings;
See what God hath done.

Are you ever burdened with a load of care?
Does the cross seem heavy you are called to bear?
Count your many blessings; ev'ry doubt will fly,
And you will be singing as the days go by.
(Chorus)

When you look at others with their lands and gold,
Think that Christ has promised you his wealth untold.
Count your many blessings; money cannot buy
Your reward in heaven nor your home on high.
(Chorus)

So amid the conflict, whether great or small,
Do not be discouraged; God is over all.
Count your many blessings; angels will attend,
Help and comfort give you to your journey's end.
(Chorus)

Text: Johnson Oatman, Jr., 1856-1922
Music: Edwin O. Excell, 1851-1921

I decided to keep a gratitude journal. I have found there is always something to be grateful for, no matter how small, and it does surprise me what the Lord has done. But being a mere mortal with human frailties, my heart still sank as I contemplated what we could do to reverse the decision that had been made for Paul.

I seemed to be forever praying for something and someone, and I often wonder how Heavenly Father coped with it all.

How can he hear and answer everyone's prayers? One day I will find out; in the meantime, I had to have faith that he was aware of me and my challenges, but I also came to realise that everyone has agency to choose. Sometimes and because of that, my prayers were not answered in the way I wanted them to be.

This was one prayer that I needed answering sooner rather than later and fasting became a necessity, and it helped me to concentrate more fully.

Our daughter offered to put together a letter on behalf of Paul, she put forth a wonderful argument as to why Paul's incapacity benefit should be reinstated.

It took eight very long months to fight the case, and was such a stressful time for all. Paul by now was put on anti-depressants.

There were many black days, and it seemed as though it would never end.

In July 2006 he was required to attend the tribunal, and with heavy hearts, we made our way to the meeting. We prayed and hoped it would be to his advantage and that hearts would be softened.

We put our case to those dealing with Paul's tribunal with our daughter as the main spokesperson. Through her questioning she was able to ascertain that they had not even read the appeal she had sent, and were not able to answer the questions which were put to them in the appeal.

We were astounded! How could they make a fair decision when they had failed to read the appeal?

They then asked me to share my feelings with them, and I did so with some emotion. I stated the mistake it would be to withdraw payment when Paul was trying to turn his life around and that he needed time to do so. I made it clear that I did not condone what had happened over the years, but that everyone needed a chance. I also said I was proud of what he was now trying to achieve. To withdraw payment now would be detrimental to him and could set him back once again.

We were told to withdraw from the room while they examined the appeal papers. I could see the mental anguish on Paul's face as we sat quietly contemplating what the outcome would be. We had done the best we could, particularly our daughter. She had spent long hours preparing for the appeal with social, medical and emotional evidence.

It was probably only minutes while waiting, but it seemed like forever. The tension was unbearable as we silently contemplated what the outcome might be. There was little indication as to their decision when they recalled us back into room.

They seemed cold and indifferent but then a change of heart.

We waited with bated breath as they seated themselves. 'Paul we have decided to reinstate your incapacity benefits after hearing your appeal, and you will receive all back payments from the date you had them stopped.'

There were tears of relief that day, and gratitude that prayers had indeed been answered. I am sure Paul wanted to cry too. We could see he was relieved and gave us a hug and expressed his gratitude for our support. He managed to keep his emotions in check and on asking if he would like to have a little lunch with us, he declined and asked to have some time to himself no doubt to reflect on the events of the day.

We felt temporarily happy and so relieved that eight months of stress had been removed, and we had hope in our hearts again. But there was more bad news for Paul when we arrived home.

His biological Dad had collapsed. He was in hospital with a suspected stroke and was currently undergoing a scan.

The diagnosis was later confirmed and it was also found that he had a lung disease. This was another setback for Paul, and it seemed as though we were no sooner over one hurdle than we were faced with another.

The children decided to have Ken, their father, transferred from Plymouth to a Nursing home in Norfolk. This relieved the pressure for them because otherwise, they would have had to make that long trip to from Cornwall on a regular basis.

On the 21st of November 2006, Mick's mother passed away following a stroke. Again, we attended another funeral and it was yet another talk for Mick to prepare. This was a time of sadness and happiness. We would miss her, but she was now at peace and for that we were grateful. Her life had been a very difficult one, and in her later years she wrote the following poem putting her feelings into words. It was later published in a book.

Thoughts

When I am on my own and all alone
I think of all the bygone days we once shared
I try to live those times again
My eyes fill with tears, some for sadness, some for joy
I liked to feel your hand in mine
And guide you where the sun would shine
And push those clouds away
We all go through stressful times
But with our love in our hearts we can pull through
Having to stay strong in our body and mind
Then say I can and I will.

Without feelings we get lost within ourselves
We begin to lose faith
Not knowing which way to turn
But with strong minds we have to guide ourselves
To take the right path to tread
It may be tough, it could be smooth
I know the right way, we have nothing to lose.
Some people get misled or misunderstood
Then life becomes difficult for them

It's the person that we are that counts
With our own thoughts we trust in ourselves to use our tact
To tell the truth is a matter of fact
We all know what we want in our thoughts
Some are successful, others distraught
But never let anyone disrupt your mind
Stay nature's way and you will find
The human way to all mankind.

Jennie Eileen Twose (Mick's Mum)

We all find different ways to express our feelings and writing poems was her way of dealing with life.

Following the funeral, Paul once again became subdued and I knew he was troubled by yet another death.

We tried to move forward again and resume some normality, but another challenge would rear its ugly head to try us *yet again.*

The Church again was my salvation and as long as I was busy, I seemed to cope. I threw myself into everything, activities, singing, giving talks, service, and teaching. Whatever came my way, I gave it my all.

Helping hands day cleaning and repainting
the benches on Gorleston seafront

Each year the Church took part in a Helping Hands service project to help in the community. This particular year we were assigned to renovate public seats which were in a very sad condition on the Gorleston seafront. As pre-arranged, we made our way to the beach clifftops where we began rubbing down the benches. I set to with such enthusiasm that I ended up with a very painful shoulder which would entail weeks of pain and immobility. But it was a very successful day with over 75 people attending. In addition to the seafront seats being renovated, weeds were dug up and pathways cleaned. I look back with fondness on all the many things I have taken part in over the years. Keeping busy was therapeutic for me.

My husband seemed to be constantly busy travelling away for work, serving as a Bishop, attending family funerals, speaking at them all and trying to support the family. He also looked after his flock, but not once did I hear him complain or bemoan his lot. Lives were touched in different ways by him, and people had great respect for him and his Christ-like nature.

He is the only member of the Church in his family, but there have been those who have been touched by the spirit and attended Church on occasions and also read The Book of Mormon. Mick's younger brother did his university thesis on The Book of Mormon and went on to earn a doctorate, but he never joined the Church but has great respect for it.

Mick's childhood was paved with thorns, but he overcame against the odds and forgave those who made his life so unhappy. He is by nature a very quiet, refined man and accepts whatever comes his way with humility and love for all.

Although none of our parents and siblings joined the Church hearts were certainly softened. Over the years, they always turned to Mick to help with funeral plans particularly giving talks and preparing the order of service programme. Even my father's heart yielded, and I remember one occasion when he and Mum came to stay with us on holiday and I invited the missionaries round for a meal. My father commented, 'What lovely young men they are! They're so polite, and if everyone lived like that, it would be a much better world.'

He wasn't one for compliments and I was taken aback that he would even suggest such a thing. I was quietly proud of our faith and could see that the more we shared our beliefs with the family, the more they came to accept our membership in the Church.

Chapter XIX –
A Testing Time

"Knowing this, that the trying of your faith worketh patience."

KJV James 1:3

Over the years during Paul's addictive periods, no one had suggested that a Hepatitis C test should be carried out. I would have thought this would be a priority. In addition to the tiredness, walking became difficult and he seemed to be struggling to do the smallest task.

Our youngest daughter advised him that he should request a hepatitis test as soon as possible to put his mind at rest. Finally Paul agreed and a few weeks later, tests were carried out and Paul nervously awaited the results. Sadly the outcome was "positive" and this was another setback for him. He became despondent again.

By this time he was feeling very ill and he shared his concerns with his care worker.

It was suggested to Paul that he should have treatment for his condition for a six month period to see if this would reverse the situation. He was warned that it would not be an easy time and there could be difficult side-effects. There was no guarantee of success. Some patients were unable to go all the way through the treatment because of the severity of these side-effects, and they often only lasted several weeks on the medicine before giving up.

Paul was worried but agreed he would give it a try. I assured him that I would be there for him at all times to see him through and give him moral support.

During this period Paul had times when he preferred to be alone but he asked me to keep in touch by phone in case he needed help.

He experienced very severe headaches, insomnia, joint pain, nausea, fatigue and fever. How he managed to keep going was hard to imagine. I worried terribly, but I was nevertheless so proud that he was determined to complete the course.

Now all we needed was to hear was that the results were good and it had all been worthwhile. Time seemed to stand still as we awaited the letter requiring us to attend the hospital to receive the news we had been waiting for.

Eventually the big day arrived, and we apprehensively made our way to the hospital to hear the results. Paul was told he should feel very proud that he had completed the course when many had given up, but the medication had failed.

I tried to hold myself together and fought back tears as I watched Paul's response. He looked so downcast and seemed to struggle to take it in. I felt helpless as I sat there trying to stay strong, but I was falling apart inside.

He sat very quietly his head bowed and then to my surprise he said, 'Can I try another course?'

My immediate response was "why"? Why would he want to go through it all again? The side-effects had been awful, and yet he was willing to go through the treatment again.

He was told very gently that they only allowed one course, so it wouldn't be possible but Paul continued to plead for another try, and she promised she would see if she could reverse the decision. It was unlikely that it would be accepted.

Within two weeks, we received the good news that Paul could undergo further treatment. This was a miracle, but I had mixed feelings nevertheless. Although I respected the decision Paul had made, but knowing what lay ahead, I was worried whether he would see it through.

So began another six months of stress and concern as he bravely underwent the unpleasant side-effects again and shut himself off from us when life became difficult.

Following the completion of the treatment, we waited for the results to arrive once again, and in August 2007 we received the news we had been waiting for. The results were clear.

We were shocked but relieved. We sat and hugged each other with me wanting to cry, but this time with relief.

Today I can still feel the joy of that day and see the relief in Paul's face. He had, at that time, overcome another hurdle.

It was as though a great cloud had been lifted once again, and Paul and I could move forward and look to the future more positively. He started to make some plans and had a great desire to take up karate again and get fit.

He sent me a card putting his feelings into words stressing that I would see a change in him in the future, and I would once again be proud of him.

This was the news I had been waiting for.

I knew it would take time, but with love and patience, there was hope at last that my son was on the right path once again.

He talked of going to college and doing a mechanical engineering course. I felt such a weight lift from me as he shared his hopes and dreams with me. Then we received further bad news.

Paul's biological Dad had sadly passed away. This meant another funeral for the family to face, and I wondered what effect this would have on Paul's emotional state.

I was soon to find out. He became withdrawn, tired and said he was on anti-depressants again. Within a short space of time Paul complained of feeling very unwell and met with his consultant who suggested that a liver biopsy should be performed.

In the meantime, further blood tests were carried out, and we once again made our way to the hospital feeling great concern that all was not well. The news confirmed my greatest fear: the virus had returned. Our hopes were dashed once again.

We were numb and sat quietly hugging as we were told the seriousness of the results we had just been given.

My heart sank. What would the biopsy reveal? More bad news?

We were told an appointment would be in approximately three months.

It seemed like forever while we waited for the letter to arrive, but no news was forthcoming. I advised Paul to see his local doctor who said he would send them a reminder.

There was still no news and our daughter Julie rang to make enquiries as to the delay. She was informed they could find no trace of a letter, and consequently they were unable to proceed.

This entailed Paul returning to the doctor and once again requesting a letter be sent as soon as possible.

Eventually, after months of delay, Paul got his appointment and Julie attended with him.

It was agreed that Paul would have a biopsy on his liver, and he would receive an appointment letter for October.

No letter arrived, so I decided to ring myself as I was anxious to know what was happening and why we had not heard.

Unfortunately I was unable to speak to the person necessary and was told by receptionist to ring back. I was given times when she would be available, and in the meantime she would pass on information I had given her regarding Paul's situation.

This I did but got an answering machine. I left my name details and reason for ringing and requested that my message be passed on to the relevant person.

Two weeks passed and still no contact whatsoever.

I rang again and this time was successful. I respectfully explained who I was and my reason for calling. She assured me she had not received any message either from receptionist or from answering machine.

Something didn't ring true.

I was then informed that Paul would not be seen in October for the biopsy as they were full, and it would now be November before he was able to be seen.

I rang Paul to pass on the message and explained all that had taken place and he sounded very ill. He thanked me for trying and asked to be left alone and not to pick him up on Sunday as usual.

Within a few days Paul received a letter with an appointment for a biopsy on October 26th and not November. It informed him he would need a blood test beforehand and he would be required to stay in hospital overnight. Previously, he was told it would be a day procedure.

Unfortunately by the time this letter had arrived, the date and time of biopsy had passed. The letter intended for Paul had been posted to the wrong address, and he had not received it until much later.

I rang the hospital and asked for an explanation, and she said she had rung me three times and left messages. None were found on our answering machine. I made it clear I could not respond if I did not receive the message.

I was then informed that a letter would be sent to Paul with another appointment with the clinic for consultation and also another letter would be sent for a biopsy.

Once again we received no news, so I rang hospital again to check when the biopsy would take place as there was some confusion. I was unable to speak in person so I left a message on the answering machine. No one got back to me.

There were so many setbacks over the next few weeks which were very frustrating. Then we received the news that Paul would not now be able to have a biopsy as they were no longer doing them. No explanation. Why?

By this time Paul's stomach was very badly swollen, and it seemed inconceivable that they would not do a biopsy to confirm why.

They now decided to do endoscopy to ascertain why he had gained so much weight.

Paul by this time was looking very ill. He was suffering with pain, sweating, headaches, mouth sores and struggling to walk.

I felt so helpless. Why were there so many delays?

We then had to face another obstacle.

Due to the abuse of drugs over the years, Paul's teeth had rotted and he would need several removed. This concerned me as I knew how ill Paul was, but the decision had to be his.

On the 8th of December he attended the dentist to have eight teeth extracted. I turned up at the surgery against his wishes and was so glad I did. He had assured me he would be fine, and he would let me know how it had gone and whether he needed any help.

He looked so ill when he came out that I wanted to cry for him. He looked shocked and said they had had to extract twelve teeth. The years of drug use had taken its toll.

He was very quiet as though in shock and struggling to walk. His mouth was bleeding badly at this point which made the situation appear so much worse.

As always, Paul was uncomplaining. I felt it important that I hid my true feelings from him and put on a brave face and tried to be as positive as possible. Outwardly I kept control and immediately phoned my husband, who was at work, to pick us up in the car and take Paul back to our home.

In spite of his condition, Paul insisted on being taken back to his home and refused our help. He promised he would telephone if he needed us.

The following day I rang as promised, and he informed me he was still in a lot of pain and unable to eat. He agreed to let me liquidise some food for him, and said he would take pain relief to ease the discomfort he was suffering.

On the 9TH of December 2008, Paul had an appointment with the hospital consultant to discuss the forthcoming endoscopy to determine his current condition. Although Paul was in no condition to attend, he felt it necessary as postponing would set him back further and delay the necessary treatment for his deteriorating condition.

Paul was continuing to put on weight around the stomach and an endoscopy was suggested to determine whether the liver was being affected or not. The consultant asked Paul to let him know if he noticed he was putting on weight around the middle.

It was pretty obvious he was, and I found it incredible that he would not have noticed that for himself.

Now, it was a matter of waiting and hoping it would not be too long before the investigation would take place for I could see that Paul was deteriorating daily.

Paul returned home and I liquidised all his food for him to ensure he was taking some nourishment to help him recover from his dental surgery.

On Saturday the 13th December 2008, I rang to find that he was still suffering and he said he could feel fragments of teeth in his gums making it difficult to eat.

I insisted he return to the dentist and get it sorted, but he was adamant that he would be alright and not to worry. How could a Mum not worry? I believe he was so tired and weary with everything that somehow could not muster up the energy to do anything about his condition. He was still suffering from fatigue and headaches and feeling unwell but insisted on being left alone.

I arranged to pick him up on Sunday following the Sacrament Service. It was a relief to have him at home with us for a short while and to ensure he had some sustenance to strengthen him a little.

It was now six days since he had his teeth extracted. Surely he should have been seeing some improvement by now? He looked gaunt and ill, and I was very concerned for him.

Over the next few days I rang him on a daily basis to let him know that he was continually in my thoughts and prayers, and the offer of help was there if needed.

Chapter XX –
Mixed Emotions

"A time to weep, and a time to laugh".

KJV Ecclesiasties 3:4

A few days before Christmas, our son Simon and his wife arrived from the United States to stay with us. The day before their arrival, Mick and I drove to the Temple and stayed overnight at the accommodation centre not far from Gatwick airport.

While we were at the Temple, we put Paul on the prayer roll.

I sat in the Temple praying and petitioning to God to hear my prayers and give me guidance for Paul and my family. It was so peaceful to sit and ponder and feel of the spirit and picture him with us in the next life with all our family around us.

How can any mother imagine life without their loved ones in the eternities?

But I knew that I could pray every hour of every day for the blessings of eternal life with my family, and no matter how I prayed or fasted and worried, my son and all my family have been given free agency. I could not take that away from them and the decisions we make have lasting consequences.

IF ONLY we had the maturity when younger to make the right choices, but life isn't like that. I look back on the many mistakes I made in my youth and regret so many things, but I was fortunate that in my later years I was able to repent and put my life in order.

How grateful I am to know that when life becomes too much, I can spend some precious time in the Temple and feel the peace and the quiet spirit that prevails in the house of the Lord.

Here within its walls we are all the same. We are all of God's children no matter what our standing in life, and I feel comforted to know here I will not be judged as the world judges. We are all in this together and need one another.

I always feel a little sad when it is time to leave the Temple. I know that I am back in the world once again and leaving behind the glimpse I have had of what eternity can be for any one of us if we commit ourselves to our Savior, Jesus Christ, and endure to the end.

The London Temple.

When we left the Temple, Mick and I drove down to Gatwick airport to wait for their arrival and found ourselves waiting hours. The plane was delayed due to inclement weather and finally detoured to arrive at Heathrow Airport where we drove on to meet them. When they went to pick up their luggage, they found that the airline had lost it en-route. What a nightmare.

On returning home I contacted Paul and he told me he was still feeling unwell but insisted he was able to cope and we were not to worry.

The following day I rang Paul again and he suggested that we didn't visit him as he was still unwell but coping and would try and visit the family over the Christmas period.

On Sunday the 21st of December, we had the children's Nativity at Church, and each year I felt touched and emotional as I watched. We had spent so many years watching our own children and grandchildren taking part, and with so many memories, it was hard not to be touched on those occasions.

Paul was still too ill to join us for lunch but stressed his need to be on his own.

The next few days were very busy preparing for Christmas day. We felt it was important for us to give quality time to our son Simon and his wife, as they were only with us for a couple of weeks before they returned home to America.

We celebrated the Christmas period without Paul but kept in touch by phone throughout.

On the 27th of December, Paul made the effort to come over and help celebrate Mick's birthday. It was actually being held a day earlier, being the Sabbath we felt it best to bring it forward a day.

No words can express how touched I was to see Paul putting in the effort when he was so ill. I could see what a strain it was to mingle in such a large family gathering and how difficult it was for him to get through the day.

He was looking so unwell that my heart went out to him, but within a couple of hours, it became apparent that Paul was unable to cope. I agreed to take him home.

When I dropped him off at his home I arranged to pick him up after Sacrament the next day, but only if he felt able to visit for lunch. I kissed him goodnight.

On Sunday, Paul was feeling very ill with a headache and high temperature and felt it best to stay away. At the time there was a lot of sickness going around which was not unusual during the winter months, and some symptoms were similar to Paul's. We agreed that it was best to avoid passing it on. But there was one difference. Paul was now experiencing nose bleeds.

On Monday I rang, and he told me he was still resting and keeping warm. He said he'd be alright, and it was probably just something he had picked up. But the signs were pointing to something more serious than a bug, and once again I pleaded with him to let me call a doctor.

On Tuesday I rang again, and this time there was no reply. This was not unusual and I had become accustomed to him not answering when he was feeling the need to isolate himself from us. He had done this for many years and would go for weeks and even months before contacting us again.

When he finally did answer, I checked that he had essentials and expressed my love for him. I also offered to pick him up if he felt able to come home, but once again he made it clear he wished to be left alone. Although he appreciated the gesture, he said he'd prefer to rest and recover before we saw him again.

But this time I couldn't get Paul out of my mind. I asked my son Simon to drive over and see if we could get access to ensure Paul was okay.

Thankfully, Paul was able to respond to Simon over the intercom and allowed him in, and was relieved to see him. He explained that he needed to pick up his methadone from the chemist but felt too ill to collect it. Simon was shocked to see how ill and weak his brother was. He saw Paul struggling for breath even walking short distances, so he understood that the medicine was needed. He offered to fetch it.

Simon did some food shopping for him and suggested he come home, but as always Paul made it clear he wanted to be at his own home.

Simon asked why he did not answer when I rang, and he explained that his mobile phone was broken. Mick and Simon then went out and purchased a new one and took it round to him. Once again, I felt a little easier knowing that I could keep in daily contact.

I kept my feelings to myself, but I was feeling very fearful that *this time* something was not right. I prayed and prayed for guidance as to what I should do. This was my son who I loved so much. We had spent so many years together facing all that came before us, and the bond we had as mother and son seemed to cement our love in a way that would confound the wisest of people.

Some would question why I could bond with my son who had let me down. But those who have been through similar trials will fully understand that the true love of a mother will rise above everything. It will forgive anything, but not condone, and that love which passeth all understanding will enable a mother to endure the unendurable if needs be and never give up.

It is important to remember that Paul had truly turned his life around. He was living a very respectable life, and he was constantly reaching out to others and helping and listening to those with challenges. Although he was used and taken for granted by some, he never sought revenge. He was resigned to the fact that this was life, and it was something he accepted.

I knew the *real* Paul and I loved him so much. And seeing him so ill pulled at my heart strings because not once did I hear him complain or feel sorry for himself.

Wednesday was the 31st of December and it was New Year's Eve. It was a time when we usually celebrated the past and welcomed in the new. I certainly didn't feel like celebrating, but I had to make it special for my visiting son and his wife.

I rang Paul to wish him a peaceful New Year but not having success sent him a text and left a message of love.

We saw in the New Year with mixed emotions and had our usual hugs and kisses. We sent messages to family who were not able to join us in person and then retired to bed.

New Year's Day dawned bright and clear and we decided on a trip to Norwich and see what the sales were offering. I phoned Paul, but there was no reply so I left a message. At the end of the day we met up with other family members and spent some time together then settled in for the night.

On Friday the 2nd of January, after a sleepless night, I arose and spent the morning catching up on chores while the family went for a drive. I was finding it hard to concentrate, and my thoughts were constantly on Paul and how he would be coping.

I kept ringing him, but each time there was no reply. I convinced myself that he was tired and asleep. The day dragged on, and it was an effort to smile and be happy because I felt so afraid that something was wrong. But I was also aware that the priority had to be the visiting family.

By the evening I was struggling to cope and suggested we call on Paul to put my mind at rest. Mick and I drive over to his home. On arriving at his flat, we rang his intercom but could not get an answer. We kept ringing but to no avail. By this time I got very worried and both Mick and I kept shouting to Paul through the letterbox 'Paul! It's Mum and Dad. Please answer.' But there was no reply.

My heart was sinking. We looked through the letterbox and saw that the lights and television were on. I felt numb and prayed quietly for guidance, but my heart told me I am too late. Mick was as distressed as I was, and we rushed to the caretaker's flat and asked for the landlord's number. We needed access permission with the spare keys, but we found out he was on holiday until Tuesday.

We then asked the caretaker to try and unlock door, as they had a set of spare keys. He tried, but it appeared that the keys didn't fit for some reason. By this time I was feeling inconsolable. This was surreal. I was in a daze but prayed in my heart for help once again.

The landlord's wife suggested that they ring another son of the landlord who should have a spare set of keys. What seemed like hours, but was in actuality a matter of minutes, he arrived. He was also unable to gain access even though the keys actually undid the lock. This was a nightmare.

We told the landlord's son and caretaker that we needed to inform the police as soon as possible. We knew our son Mark, a policeman, was on duty and I wanted him to be aware of the situation first. I was not sure how to contact him personally, so I rang our ex son-in-law, Mark, also a policeman, and pleaded for his help in contacting our son and getting assistance as soon as possible. He sounded in shock but promised that he would contact Mark as a matter of urgency.

It must have been only minutes, but it seemed like forever before we heard the police sirens. Our son Mark had arrived with his companion.

What a difficult task for him. Dealing with traumatic situations in the line of duty is something that the police have to deal with on a regular basis, but when one's own family is involved, it is doubly difficult. He ran past us as we stood traumatised on the stairs and started banging on the door and shouting to Paul. There was no reply. He tried the keys again unsuccessfully and then realised that Paul probably had a lock or bolt on the inside of the door for extra security.

He explained that they would have to break the door in but would need to call someone in authority to do so with the right equipment. Within minutes help was at hand and it seemed as though there were people everywhere, outside the door, on the stairs, in the hallway and I wanted to scream to them all, 'Go away! It's my son. Just let me in.'

I stood in shock and waited as the police broke the door down. Mark rushed in to find Paul lying on the bathroom floor. It was too late. He was dead.

I tried to enter but was gently advised by Mark, 'Mum, Dad don't go in. He's gone. Go home.' I insisted I wanted to see him, but Mark advised me again that we should go home and be with the family.

I felt inconsolable to think Paul had been lying there alone and might have suffered before he died. **IF ONLY** I had been there for him to give him one last hug and tell him how much I loved him. I would later regret not having done so.

Six months following his biological Dad's death, Paul, my lovely son was found dead.

As we left to return home, we found the street outside Paul's flat filled with people who had heard the sirens and come out of their houses to see what was happening. I found the whole experience unreal as though it was happening to someone else and I was an onlooker.

As Mick drove, I could see the emotion he was feeling. He was trying to hold it all together, but he was so emotional and crying. I had never seen him cry like this before. I am sure he was driving on auto pilot, as we both tried to make sense of it all.

We now had the difficult task of letting the family know, and I felt my whole body shaking as I prepared to tell them the very sad news.

I rang our children as we drove home. I told them as gently as I could that Paul had passed away, and we would meet with them in our home soon to comfort one another.

I have no need to describe the scene as our family

gathered together. We sat sometimes in silent grief, and at other times completely unable to contain our tears, as we poured out our very souls.

A policewoman came and took statements, and it was very late before everyone returned to their own homes. When they did, an eerie silence settled within the walls of our home.

Mick by now was mentally and physically tired. He went to bed leaving me to sit and ponder on the events of the evening. Sleep was not an option, and at 3:00am, unable to momentarily shut my eyes, I drove down to the beach passing my daughter's house on the way. Her lights were still on and I felt so tempted to knock on her door and for us to comfort each other, but I held back. I wasn't sure whether she had retired but had left the lights on to give her some feeling of security at such a difficult time.

I had spent many nights alone when Mick has working away and had always left a light on at night for comfort, and I assumed being a single Mum that this is what she had done too. I reluctantly drove on, stopping at the beach and talking to God in prayer and pleading for comfort.

On arriving home again, I wrote in my journal about the events of the day. I described the sadness of my son's death and how I wished I had been there for him in his last hours.

Somehow I managed to survive without sleep and faced the new day still not fully able to take it all in.

Where could there be a little peace away from this nightmare?

Chapter XXI –
Peace Before The Storm

"Where can I turn for peace"?

Title of a hymn by Emma Lou Thayne

I drove down to the Church and sat quietly in the chapel. I prayed to Heavenly Father and told him how terribly sad I felt at losing my son. Suddenly there came a feeling of peace. I realised no one knew better than he did of my suffering, as he too had seen his son suffer and die in such a way that I would never be able to fully comprehend.

I tried to keep my emotions as controlled as possible in the days ahead. This was not only for my sake, but for my children and grandchildren. I also knew I had much to do in the days and weeks ahead.

Saturday January 3rd 2009

I've thought of Mum today. It would have been her birthday, and I look back on her life and think how difficult it had been for her in many ways. Seeing her suffering in her last days from Alzheimer's was not easy, and I felt at peace knowing that she was now free from the trials of this life and reunited with her loved ones. Paul loved her. I am happy in the knowledge that he was with her now.

I am feeling physically ill today, hot and cold with a temperature, but I soldiered on. Our son Simon and his wife feel unwell too, so hopefully it is just a virus going around.

Sunday 4th January 2009

I haven't been to Church today as feeling too ill. Mick has gone as he is Bishop and has so much to do, but I am sure it will be a struggle for him to get through the morning.

Mark has gone home to be with his family although he is estranged from his wife He's finding everything difficult to deal with right now. It has been a very challenging time for him, and of course, for all the family.

Monday 5th January 2009

I went to Paul's flat today with Mick and Simon to sort Paul's clothes etc. Simon became upset as he had had a very close bond with Paul. It was hard to contain our emotions as we went through Paul's possessions and packed away what we could.

We had arranged to meet with the landlord, so that he could assess condition of flat and come to some agreement as to what we could leave or dispose of. He was very matter of fact and showed little concern about our situation but was more interested in who was going to pay for the damage to the broken lock on the door.

He could see we were distressed, but the door was his priority. How very sad.

Tuesday 6th January 2009

Julie, Kenny, Mick and I went back to Paul's flat to wash and clean everything before the landlord came for a final inspection.

Very little was said as we laboriously cleaned each room, Julie having taken on the task of cleaning the bathroom where Paul had been found, to make sure I did not have to view the situation.

Paul was a devoted Manchester United fan, and Simon asked if he could keep Paul's football top. He wanted to frame it and take back home when he returned to America. Unfortunately, we mislaid it, and realised we must have put it in with other items and taken to the refuse tip.

We went with haste to the tip and tried sifting through the mounds of bags but with little success. We thanked the person in charge, and he promised he would do his best to find the top. He suggested that we returned in an hour.

Sadly, when we arrived we were unable to find the man.

We resigned ourselves to the fact that it had been lost, but we had only driven a short distance when we viewed a car flashing his lights at us to pull over.

We assumed we had done something wrong, but that wasn't the case. The driver pulled up, opened his window and gave us the Manchester top which he had managed to find amongst the hundreds of bags ready for being transported to those in need.

What a lovely man and so considerate! What a contrast to the rich landlord whose main concern was who was going to pay for a new lock.

My faith in human nature was restored.

The coroner visited with us and said the tests on Paul were inconclusive. His liver had been giving up. He also had an ulcer, hepatitis, double pneumonia and other symptoms, but as the tests were inconclusive, more in-depth tests were needed. These would be much more involved and traumatic. The choice was ours. As far as I was concerned, my son was dead. I wanted him to now rest in peace, and maybe in the next life, I would know the truth.

No other results would change what had happened.

The coroner said he wasn't surprised at my reaction, as he knew my beliefs and my faith in the afterlife. He was such a lovely man and very comforting.

Wednesday 7th January 2009
Today we were so busy. Met with the landlord who was satisfied with cleanliness of flat and said he would be in touch for refund of deposit which had been paid in advance. We never received it.

We passed over the keys and walked sadly away for the last time. We paused for a brief glance back before we drove away taking memories that will stay in our hearts forever.

Went and sorted out a wreath for funeral then met with funeral directors.

Made numerous phone calls but unable to get through to many of them.

Thursday 8th January 2009
I was still so ill but have been trying to fight it, as there was

so much to do. I had a very high temperature, it was painful to cough and I've had bad headaches. Breathing was difficult.

My daughter Julie popped in, and having seen the state of my health, insisted I see the doctor. He diagnosed pneumonia and very low blood pressure and told me I needed to go home and straight back to bed.

I was told that if I was no better by Sunday, I was to call the doctor immediately. I explained that it wasn't possible to rest. I had just lost my son and his funeral was on Tuesday and there was so much to do. He firmly told me if I did not rest it could be my funeral too.

That was a wakeup call for me, and I promptly took myself off to bed, but worrying how on earth I would cope with so much to do in such a short time.

How grateful I am for the Priesthood in my life. My son Simon, assisted by Mick, administered to me and promised me I would be well enough to attend Paul's funeral and fully recover.

I had a very bad night but tried to keep in mind the promise given to me that all would be well. I knew Heavenly Father was aware of my needs at this time and would be there to give me comfort.

It was a week since Paul's body was found and I still felt so lost. I knew Paul was away from the mortal pains of this world and not suffering now, and I am grateful for that.

I was getting so weary and tired with the worry of it all, and for Paul's sake as well as mine, I must accept what has happened and be grateful for the years we had together.

Oh Paul, how I loved you.

Saturday 10th 2009
I was still in bed feeling ill, coughing and finding it difficult to breathe. I was very frustrated.

I had family staying here and they have had to look after me, but I must build up my strength for the funeral on Tuesday.

Sunday 11th January.
I was unable to go to Church today so my husband Mick held the fort and tried to cope as husband, father and Bishop.

He has been so supportive and I could not wish for a better husband and father.

Monday 12ᵗʰ January 2009

Although tired and week, I felt better.

Family members arrived for the funeral and cards were coming through the door thick and fast.

I was not sure I could face it all. Coping with any death of a loved one was painful enough, but because of the circumstances related to Paul's death, the situation was worse. Over a short period of time we have had six family funerals but nothing can compare with the loss of a son in this way.

I was grateful for Mick's place of work. They had been so supportive and shown great compassion when others have failed to do so.

And at times like this we find out who our true friends are. I am sure there were those who have wanted to express their condolences but due to circumstances found it difficult to do so and passed by on the other side.

Tomorrow was looming. How shall I deal with it? Only time would tell.

Tuesday 13ᵗʰ January 2009

What a night it has been. I was struggling to come to terms with my loss and kept torturing myself with the IF ONLY that seemed to keep raising its ugly head and fill my every thought.

Morning came as a welcome relief, and I rose from my bed to prepare for the funeral. The family gathering was to be in our home. Food had to be prepared in advance, and all rallied round to ensure there was sufficient to sustain and warm those attending on a cold and wintry day.

The dreaded moment arrived, and we made our way to the Church with very heavy hearts. It all seemed unreal as though it was happening to someone else and I seemed to function on automatic pilot.

Mick conducted the service and I could see the pain in his face as he stood and welcomed all to the remembrance service of Paul.

As we stood and sang the opening hymn "All Things Bright and Beautiful" I felt as though my legs were about to give way and my heart break. Outwardly I tried to control my emotions not wanting others to see me cry as by nature I am a private person and prefer to weep within the confines of my home but it was such a struggle.

Our son-in-law gave the opening prayer and I am sure it was difficult for him too as he would have been celebrating his birthday today in different circumstances. Shortly after Paul's funeral, he would have to face the untimely death of his father too and take an active part in his service.

My husband read the Eulogy which must have been a struggle for him, but he was able to keep his emotions under control. I am sure all were moved as Paul's life was shared with those who were present.

Following the eulogy our oldest daughter Karen read a poem written by our daughter Julie who felt unable to.

Paul

On a night in 65
Amidst a thunderstorm
Through pain and tears and many fears,
A baby boy was born.

His family loved him dearly
For he was a bonnie boy,
With his cheeky sense of humour
He brought them so much joy.

Then one day when he was older
He took a path he did not know,
But it led to only heartache
He knew not where to go.

But his loved ones stood right by him
And led him by the way
They knew one day he'd turn around
And they waited for that day.

Many years went by
And troubles were many
But still they stood by his side
And over time
With love and patience
The space between them seemed less wide.

And then a man
Mature in thought
He saw a better way,
Renewed in heart he gave his love
To all who came his way.

But the road had done its damage
And his body took the toll
Till finally he "gave up the ghost"
When God said "Come home Paul"

And so although we'll miss you
More than words could ever say
We know with faith we'll see you
In Paradise some day

Until then we'll carry on
And do the best we can
But someday, like you, we'll leave this earth
And discard the mortal man.

For all of us must walk this way
And life's lessons we must learn
Until Celestial we can be
When homeward we return.

Together then forever
With no more hurt or pain
And in His love we'll find His peace
With God's eternal plan.

Julie Hearn

Our son Simon then shared some personal thoughts and expressed his love for Paul and shared the following poem.

Beyond Life's Gateway

There's an open gate
At the end of the road
Through which each must go alone
And there in a light we cannot see
Our Father claims his own
Beyond the gate, your loved one
Finds happiness and rest,
And there is comfort in the thought
That a loving God knows best.

Author Unknown

The closing hymn was "God Be with You Till We Meet Again" and then we left the Church to the strains of Eric Clapton singing "Tears in Heaven".

I am sure it was with great difficulty that he sang this song dedicated to his son who sadly lost his life through a tragic accident. Beautiful words beautifully sung.

The journey to the graveside seemed slow and endless and this was for me the hardest part of the day, when reality started to sink in and I quietly whispered "I love you" as the final committal prayer was given and we gathered together united in our grief and laid Paul to rest.

The rest of the day followed in a blur and it was such a relief when we had said our goodbyes to family and friends and I was able to retire to my room and let out my innermost feelings.

The night was a long one.

The following morning Mick, myself, Simon and his wife travelled down to the Temple where I found some peace and comfort although I am crying inside.

But what better place could I be than here away from the pains of the world?

Thursday 15th January 2009

Today at Gatwick airport we said our goodbyes to Simon and his wife who are flying home to America. What a wrench it was to say farewell in such sad circumstances when they had so looked forward to a Christmas holiday with us.

I felt such pain within me as they hugged and kissed us and walked forlornly through the gates of the departure lounge.

Very little was said as Mick and I made our way home once again, but words were not needed.

The days ahead were difficult with many phone calls to make, forms to fill in and much to be done alongside trying to return to normal life again.

On Sunday we attended Church but even that was difficult to deal with, listening to the talks that centered on death and sorrow.

On Monday Mick resumed work but returned home early and in pain with back problems, a recurring problem for him.

Three weeks after Paul's death I wrote in my journal and put my feeling into words.

Paul you would hate to be back here. The world is in turmoil and people are losing their jobs, homes and their hope.

You are in the best place, and I pray that you are remembering the years here and the love you had for the gospel when you were young.

I am so looking forward to being sealed to you and can look forward to a happy reunion with you again one day.

I can't express how much I want to be with you and the family in the next life, and I want you to be a special part of that.

I know you took a wrong path while here on earth and I worried and fretted not knowing what your eternal destiny would be, but I have been comforted by the words of Joseph Smith the Prophet who gave such wonderful hope to me when I read his words.

The Prophet Joseph Smith declared and he never taught a more comforting doctrine that the eternal sealing's of faithful parents and the divine promises made to them for valiant service in the Cause of Truth, would save not only themselves but likewise their posterity.

"Though some of the sheep may wander, the eye of the Shepherd is upon them. And sooner or later they will feel the tentacles of Divine Providence reaching out after them and drawing them back to the fold. Either in this life or the world to come, they will return. They will have to pay for their debt to justice; they will suffer for their sins; and may tread a thorny path; but if it leads them at last, like the penitent Prodigal, to a loving and forgiving father's heart, the painful experience will not have been in vain. Pray for your careless and disobedient children; hold on to them with your faith. Hope on, trust on, till you see the Salvation of God"

(Taken from an Ensign talk given by Orson F. Whitney April 1929)

What comforting words and yet I still have times when in spite of gospel truths I still question myself and inwardly think

IF ONLY.

The days ahead were painful.

Having to return to Paul's flat, collect mail, sort out bills to be paid, and coping with my Church commitments as well as supporting my grieving family and not having my husband beside me as he was working away again was so very difficult.

But keeping busy was so important during the grieving process.

I tried to get some normality back into my life, did my visiting teaching and gave my support as counselor to my Relief Society President as best as I could but I struggled to maintain the smiling countenance that others were used to seeing.

I visited some of Paul's friend's, and although some had taken the wrong path in life, I found them to be truly sincere in their love for Paul. They were all lovely people and spoke with genuine emotion as they related their relationship and friendship they had had with Paul over the years. All expressed that Paul was a very special person who had touched all of their lives for good.

I learned a great deal from those visits, and it comforted me to hear from them the many kindnesses Paul had shown to them over the years.

One gift that I was very aware of and had confirmed was his forgiving nature.

He never bore a grudge although he had many times when it would have been understandable had he done so.

I believe my experiences over the years with those who have not perhaps taken the path that most people travel, has given me the ability to understand others whose lives are sometimes frowned upon and are judged harshly and there are many who would rather walk on the "other side" than reach out with love and compassion and try to understand the reasons that people stray from the path that would be considered the "norm"

We are all imperfect beings, and although we may not commit some of the more serious sins in life, we all sin at times in different ways. I love the hymn "Lord, I Would Follow Thee".

Within the words of that hymn stand out the feelings I have for those who may feel downtrodden in life by others.

Lord, I Would Follow Thee

Savior, may I learn to love thee,
Walk the path that thou hast shown,
Pause to help and lift another,
Finding strength beyond my own.
Savior, may I learn to love thee
Lord, I would follow thee.

Who am I to judge another
When I walk imperfectly?
In the quiet heart is hidden
Sorrow that the eye can't see.
Who am I to judge another?
Lord, I would follow thee.

I would be my brother's keeper;
I would learn the healer's art.
To the wounded and the weary
I would show a gentle heart.
I would be my brother's keeper
Lord, I would follow thee.

Savior, may I love my brother
As I know thou lovest me,
Find in thee my strength, my beacon,
For thy servant I would be.
Savior, may I love my brother
Lord, I would follow thee.

Lord I Would Follow Thee
by (lyricist: Susan Evans McCloud, b. 1945
Composer: K. Newell Dayley, b. 1939)
© by Intellectual Reserve, Inc

Although we were still grieving, we would soon have the added stress of a divorce looming with one of our children. The timing was terrible and very distressing for our son, Mark, who had sadly found Paul's body and had been badly affected by it.

My heart went out to him.

I felt I was being tried on all levels, and every day brought some new challenge which needed great strength and fortitude to overcome.

Prayer was essential, and I pleaded with Heavenly Father

to give me strength to stay faithful no matter what I would need to face in the future. Little did I realise that my challenges would be ongoing, and I would need all my strength physically, spiritually and mentally in the days and years that lay ahead of me.

In April 2009 I was released as a counselor in Relief Society and called as counselor in Primary. I felt very shocked, as I had only had weeks to grieve, but I determined to give of my best to the calling.

Previous to Paul's death our friend who was an entertainer and performed as Elvis at our Relief Society Social had received news that his son who had gone missing had been found dead.

We couldn't believe what had happened. He had been abducted taken to an isolated spot, doused with petrol and set on fire.

We had tried to help them cope with their son's death and spent many hours talking and listening, as they related the terrible details to us. It was one of the hardest things I have found myself having to do.

We attended the funeral, which because of the circumstance was very public, and we spent some heart-wrenching weeks visiting with them in their time of sorrow.

I know when we are in the service of others, it helps to lessen our own sorrow. They were sincerely grateful for our visits as they shared their innermost feelings with us. We continued to meet with them on a regular basis but the father was steadily going downhill. He was a shadow of his former self.

Life became so difficult for them that they moved away not leaving a forwarding address to start a new life. I will never forget how this terrible tragedy changed their life forever.

I am very grateful for the strength they gave to me, and the knowledge that all around us are those who are facing trials and challenges too and that I am not alone.

"Missing someone gets easier every day because even though it is one day further from the last time you saw each other, it is one day closer to the next time you will".

Chapter XXII -
Our Time in Ireland

"Success in what we do may be desperately important to others"

Author Unknown

During this time Mick was asked by the directors of his company if he would be willing to go to Ireland for a month to evaluate a small firm acquired by the company, which he did with my blessing.

He returned home, gave his report to the directors, and made recommendations for the company to progress. They then asked Mick if he would be willing to work in Ireland as the manager of the company; they would provide suitable housing, pay for all utilities etc. and that I would be able to go with him. We would be able to return home occasionally from a few days to a week on expenses.

They also suggested that he take me over to Ireland for a week to see if I liked it and then decide whether Mick should take up their proposal.

We sat down and discussed in depth what the directors had suggested and what would be required.

This was a time for fasting and prayer to decide whether we should stay in England, as Mick was still Bishop, or to move and work and serve in another Ward.

By this time he had already been serving for almost six years as Bishop. We fasted and prayed and the answer was very clear. We both felt we were needed in Ireland and we could also serve an unofficial mission while there.

This feeling was too strong to ignore, and within a few days, we made our journey to Ireland hoping that we would receive an answer as to the final decision we should make.

Mick was required to work in the office, but we also needed time to find a home

We both felt good about everything, and returned home feeling at peace and hoping our time in Ireland would be fruitful. Mick made his return journey back to Ireland to commence managing the company and finalise our accommodation ready for the move.

He found a suitable house to rent, made the necessary arrangements and then returned home.

On the 29th of July, we left for Galway, on the west coast of Ireland, and said our goodbyes to family and friends. This was a difficult time for me. I wanted to be at home and support my family who were still grieving, but I could not ignore the promptings I had received. We travelled by car to Holyhead in Anglesey and then took a ferry to Dublin. We stayed overnight there in a hotel before travelling to our new home.

We arrived tired and weary and spent the rest of the day settling in, shopping for food and other essentials.

Our new home was a modern house in a small cul-de-sac which overlooked the beautiful Galway Bay. It was a lovely location and we soon got to know the local residents who were very friendly and welcoming.

We attended a Church in Galway where there were approximately 35 members. Although small in number, it did not detract from the spirit and I felt very comfortable and at peace. We settled in and determined to give our all to the Church and serve to the best of our ability.

Our Branch President warmly welcomed us both, and to our surprise, we learned he had served a mission in Leeds at the same time as our son Mark. They had even spent some time together. His wife served as a missionary too, and she had also met Mark during her time in England. He expressed his sadness at the news of our son's death and then related he had lost his brother too and in sad circumstances before we arrived.

We were taken aback by this news but felt comforted to know that we would be supported by them during our time in Ireland, and they would understand that our emotions were still very raw.

I was quickly called as a counselor in Relief Society and

found not only was I required to serve in this capacity but also to teach, arrange Homemaking evenings, do Visiting Teaching and Compassionate Service. I was also called as a Branch Missionary.

*Me with some of the Galway Branch sisters
celebrating our Relief Society birthday social.*

Mick was called as counselor to the Branch President, and within a couple of weeks, he was also called to be the Branch Mission Leader. He taught lessons in Sunday School and Priesthood on a regular basis. It was quite a shock receiving these callings, but it confirmed our feelings that this is where we needed to be at this time.

On Sunday, the meetings started at 11am until 2pm. and we also found ourselves away from home for seven hours as Council and Missionary meetings were also held on Sundays. This was to eliminate travelling during the week as many of the members lived long distances from the Church.

I truly felt the spirit during our time of service in Ireland and so loved our calling in the Missionary programme.

In all there were six other missionaries, two of which were a mature couple, and as we welcomed them into our home for meals and meetings our testimonies were strengthened and my spirit was strong.

They were very special days.

We were so very busy especially Mick who had much to accomplish in his employment and also give of his time in the Church.

We spent many hours visiting less active members, and each day was full as we prepared lessons, firesides and spoke in the Sacrament.

I remember being asked to give a Relief Society presentation in Sacrament one Sunday and decided to base it on the Savior. We sang a beautiful song. "If The Savior Stood Beside Me" and I remember the emotions we felt, and the spirit touching our hearts as we expressed our love for the Savior in song.

The words were very poignant and centered on how we would act if Christ was standing beside us. What would we say? Would we continue doing the things we did?

No doubt we would sometimes do things differently.

As with all things in life there is a time when we have to move on. In the summer of 2010 when our time was up in Ireland, we said our sad farewells to our friends and returned to England. We had seen some of the fruits of our labors and witnessed the return of less active members and some baptisms. It was a wrench to leave behind such a lovely little Branch and some very special friends.

I will never forget the bonds of friendship that were formed and the love that was manifested to us during our time there. It also gave me the strength to keep going after the untimely death of my son. Keeping busy was the best way of dealing with my grief and taught me true love and empathy for others. Not that I did not already possess that quality, but it truly brought home to me the words "When ye are in the service of your fellow men ye are only in the service of your God".

I felt we had served a mission in our own way.

I remember one sister, who I befriended, struggling because of the challenges she was experiencing at the time. She was very negative and questioned why her life was so hard. I tried to help her soften her heart and grew to love her, and as she attended some events, I could see a change for the better.

But soon after we left for home she made the decision to leave the Church. I felt great sadness that she had tried but failed to cope with the challenges she was facing. I kept in touch and hoped and prayed she would have a change of heart and would realise the mistake she was making. Time passed and then, out of the blue, I received a letter to say she had been sitting in Church one Sunday and listening to a sister who was giving a talk and she had expressed her feelings that we all had a guardian angel, and as my friend listened she said she knew her guardian was me! She sent a lovely letter expressing her love and thanks to me. That meant so much to me. Just to know she had returned to her faith was such a heartwarming experience, and I knew my time in Ireland had not been wasted.

Mick continued to manage the company from England but travelled to Ireland on a monthly basis.

In October 2011, following a very stressful period, he suffered a complete breakdown. I received a distressed phone call from him. His voice was breaking as he related to me that he could not take the pressure anymore and waited for my response.

I assured him that I would support him and get help to him as soon as possible. These were difficult days, and he retired from work shortly afterwards. I will not dwell on his breakdown, but looking back now, we can see a purpose for this happening too.

From this trial came a blessing coming to fruition much later when events made it possible for him to give compassionate service to another loved one who was in desperate need and also nearing a breakdown. If he had still been working, that would not have been possible. Early retirement enabled him to spend three months with our son in America, trying to give comfort and support to him in his time of need, and for that, I am so very grateful.

IF ONLY we could have seen ahead, but then we would not have needed faith. We need to have faith without the sign to prove our belief in him who knows best.

I remember many years ago my daughter-in-law giving a lesson on Faith one Sunday and at the end she gave out a little picture of the Savior and on it were the words.

"BELIEVE ME FOR THE VIEW UP HERE IS VERY CLEAR

TRUST ME FOR I CAN SEE CLEARLY OVER THE NEXT HILL"

I have never forgotten those words.

I truly believe the Savior is aware of every one of us and can see ahead of us, but he allows us to experience the trials of this mortal life because that is the plan.

Chapter XXIII - Moving On

Albert Einstein

As my life moves forward, I thank my Heavenly Father for the Gospel here on earth, for the truths I have learned and the knowledge that: I know where I came from, why I am here and the opportunity I have of returning to him if I am faithful.

I have also come to know of the reality of the adversary and their existence because I have had to endure persistent pressure on me through the trials and temptations that have been my lot here on earth.

During my life here, I have experienced physical, emotional, and mental pain that I would not have chosen.

My challenges continue and I now have to live for the day and hope for tomorrow. But I will no doubt continue to echo the words **IF ONLY** as I press on with my life and hope eternal victory will be mine with those I love beside me.

There are those who say we should be grateful for our trials when some have not had to experience a great many themselves.

I cannot say I am grateful for mine, but I am grateful for the strength I have been given to face them and still stay on the right path.

This scripture has helped me so much when I have been feeling down.

"My peace I leave with you my peace I give unto you, not as the world giveth, give I unto you, let not your heart be troubled neither let it be afraid"

John 14: 27

I believe this scripture is telling me I can have inner peace within my heart if I hold on to my faith.

I can say in all honesty I have never blamed God for my trials because so many of them have come about through unwise choices or unavoidable circumstances. We have to suffer the consequences of them either directly or indirectly.

Do I still miss my son? Of course I do every day, but I know Paul would want me to be happy and remember the good times we shared together.

I must share with you a poem.

IF ONLY

(written by my daughter Julie as if it was written by Paul)

If I could see you now
I'd tell you I'm okay
I'd hold you close within my arms
And wipe your tears away

If I could show you now
The things that I can see,
You'd be amazed, your heart would swell
And you'd be glad for me.

If I could tell you now
Of the progress that I've made
Of all the things I'm learning
And the laws that I've obeyed

If you could see the place I'm in
With loved ones we hold dear,
Your soul would fill with love and joy
To know that they were near.

If you could feel the peace and warmth
That I feel every day
You'd never want me to come back,
You'd want me here to stay.

If I could have you with me now
That choice I wouldn't make,
For there are those who need you more
So stay there for their sake.

If I could draw the veil right back,
And show you where I am,
Then on this day you'd celebrate
Our Heavenly Fathers Plan.

If you could find it in you
To try this day to smile
Just knowing that I'm happy
And that I'll see you in a while.

If we could just both focus
On eternal matters now,
And leave the rest behind us
Then before His knee we'll bow.

If I could ask you just one thing
It's happy that you'll be,
For although we miss each other
One day you'll be with me.

And if I could give thanks for anything
Before that day will come,
The thing that I'm most thankful for
Is that you are my Mum.

I LOVE YOU
PAUL X

There are days when I feel I am moving on and cope so well that I start to feel guilty. Then there are days when I feel I can't go on, but I do the best I can and that is all I am capable of.

There are so many things I cannot change that have an effect on me. Just listening to others talking with pride in Sacrament meetings about their children, their achievements, and seeing young men passing the Sacrament and picturing Paul when he was their age performing the same ordinance. That is hard.

IF ONLY Paul had stayed the course, had a career, served a Mission, married had children, life could have been so different.

But here I am still wishing, still hoping, and praying that all will be well **IF ONLY** I keep on the Lord's side of the line and not wander into paths that would lead me astray.

Chapter XXIV – My Faith In The Gospel of Jesus Christ

"Hope is to believe there will be a good outcome"

Author Unknown

Life continues to be challenging. There are many new family situations that continue to test one to the limit at times. I have no doubt they will continue, but with God's help I hope I can overcome and be able to say one day as Paul did in 2nd Timothy v7 "I have fought a good fight, I have finished my course, I have kept the faith".

I hope by sharing my story with you that no matter where you find yourself, you too will find strength each day and determine, that with God's help and through his son Christ's atoning sacrifice that you will remember the pain and sorrow he endured for us which we cannot comprehend right now. All that we can do right now is live by faith and hope for tomorrow. That is all Christ expects of us. We do not know what tomorrow may bring, yet we continue to fret instead of doing what we can to improve our lives here and now.

But perfection comes little by little, precept by precept, and it is only by improving our lives daily and determining to be better today than we were yesterday that we can progress and move on.

If we continue to concentrate on the **IF ONLY** we cannot hope to move forward, and we will still continue to live in the past which will only hinder our progress and hold us back from achieving our ultimate goal here on earth. To be with those we love who are now beyond the veil, and live with Heavenly Father and his son Jesus Christ.

That should be the most important goal for all of us and I cannot wait to hear my Savior welcome me on that final day and say "Well done thou good and faithful servant"!

Not **IF ONLY.**

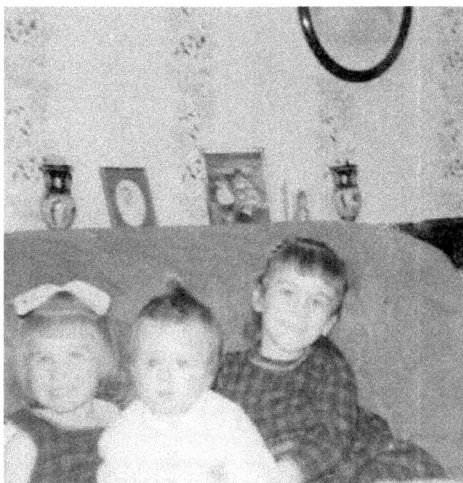

Paul with his sisters Karen and Julie

Paul with baby brother Mark

Paul enjoying the broads with us

Glossary of Terms

"Knowledge is extremely important for it will be useful someday"

Michael Colley

Mormon(s): Mormons are members of The Church of Jesus Christ of Latter-day Saints. Mormon is one of the prominent Prophets found in the Book of Mormon.

KJV: King James Version of the Holy Bible.

Book of Mormon: The Book of Mormon is a book of scripture used by The Church of Jesus Christ of Latter-day Saints, which adherents believe contains writings of ancient Prophets who lived on the American continent from approximately 2200 BC to AD 421. The Book of Mormon is a second witness to Jesus Christ, the first being the Holy Bible.

Doctrine and Covenants: The Doctrine and Covenants is a collection of divine revelations and inspired declarations given for the establishment and regulation of the kingdom of God on the earth in the last days. Although most of the sections are directed to members of The Church of Jesus Christ of Latter-day Saints, the messages, warnings, and exhortations are for the benefit of all mankind and contain an invitation to all people everywhere to hear the voice of the Lord Jesus Christ, speaking to them for their temporal well-being and their everlasting salvation.

Pearl of Great Price - Moses and Abraham: The Pearl of Great Price is part of the canonical standard works of The Church of Jesus Christ of Latter-day Saints.
"The Pearl of Great Price is a selection of choice materials touching many significant aspects of the faith and doctrine of The Church of Jesus Christ of Latter-day Saints. These items were produced by Joseph Smith Jr. and were published in the Church periodicals of his day."

Aaronic Priesthood: The Aaronic Priesthood also called the Priesthood of Aaron or the Levitical Priesthood is the lesser of the two orders of Priesthood recognised as an order of Priesthood in the Church of Jesus Christ of Latter Day Saints.

Melkizedek Priesthood: The Melchizedek Priesthood is the greater of the two orders of Priesthood recognised in the Church of Jesus Christ of Latter Day Saints.

Relief Society: The Relief Society is an educational women's organisation and an official auxiliary of The Church of Jesus Christ of Latter-day Saints. It was founded in 1842 in Nauvoo, Illinois, USA and has over 6 million members in over 170 countries.

Primary: The Primary is a children's organisation and an official auxiliary within The Church of Jesus Christ of Latter-day Saints. It acts as a Sunday school organisation for the Church's children under the age of 12.

Joseph Smith: Joseph Smith was the first President and Lord's Prophet of the Church of Jesus Christ of Latter Day Saints.

Word of Wisdom: The Word of Wisdom is a health code which is found in section 89 of the Doctrine and Covenants.

Young Men: The Young Men is a male youth organisation for 12-18 year olds and an official auxiliary of The Church of Jesus Christ of Latter-day Saints.

Young Women: The Young Women is a youth organisation for 12-18 year olds and an official auxiliary of The Church of Jesus Christ of Latter-day Saints.

Temple Marriage: Celestial marriage also called the New and Everlasting Covenant of Marriage, Eternal Marriage or Temple Marriage is a doctrine of The Church of Jesus Christ of Latter-day Saints. Whereas ordinary marriage is for "until death do you part", Temple marriage is for time and all eternity.

Ward/Branch: The Church of Jesus Christ of Latter-day Saints local congregations are called Wards (or Branches for smaller congregations). They are organised geographically and members attend a Ward or Branch near their home. The Ward in this book refers to the chapel in Gorleston, Norfolk. The Branch refers to the meeting house in Galway, Ireland.

Stake: A group of Wards and Branches forms a stake, and the leader of a stake is a stake president. "Stake" is not a term found in the New Testament, but is taken from Old Testament tent imagery in which the "tent," or Church, is held up by supporting stakes (see KJV Isaiah 54:2).

Temple: In The Church of Jesus Christ of Latter-day Saints a Temple is a building dedicated to be a House of the Lord, and they are considered by Church members to be the most sacred structures on earth. Upon completion, Temples are usually open to the public for a short period of time ("Open House"). During the Open House, the Church conducts tours of the Temple with missionaries and members from the local area serving as tour guides, and all rooms of the Temple are open to the public. The Temple is then dedicated as a "House of the Lord", after which only members who are deemed worthy are permitted entrance. Thus, they are not Churches (meetinghouses) but rather sacred places of worship. To date there are currently 143 throughout the world and Temple building is ongoing.

Seminary: Seminary is a worldwide, four-year religious educational program for youth ages 14 through 18. It is operated by The Church of Jesus Christ of Latter-day Saints but is open to teenagers of all faiths.

Institute: Institutes of Religion provide religious educational classes for young single adults aged 18 through 30 and university students who belong to The Church of Jesus Christ of Latter-day Saints but is also open to single adults of all faiths.

Setting Apart: A "Setting apart" is a Priesthood ordinance that is performed by the laying on of hands, authorising a man or woman to serve in a Church calling. It occurs after one has been sustained by common consent to perform certain duties and responsibilities in a specific calling in a geographical or organisational part of the Church. It is performed by, or under the direction of, the one in authority over that unit. One is "ordained" to Priesthood offices, but is "set apart" to preside or serve. In the setting apart, one is given the authority and charged to act; he or she is also counseled, instructed, and blessed. The blessings are conditional upon faithful performance.

Visiting Teacher: Visiting teaching is an organised means whereby the women of the Church receive regular instructional and compassionate service visits-usually by personal contact in the home-from other female members of the Church. The purpose is to promote sisterhood, present inspirational messages, and note instances of need wherein the temporal and spiritual resources of the Church might be helpful.

Home Teacher: Home teaching is a responsibility of Priesthood holders in The Church of Jesus Christ of Latter-day Saints and is designed to allow families to be taught in their own homes, in addition to weekly Church services. Every family/individual are assigned two Priesthood holders to friendship and visit on a regular basis to present spiritual messages and help with the temporal needs of the household. This is a very powerful, moving and emotional book which is well written and straightforward, yet sensitive and flowing.

About the author

Elizabeth Colley was born in Great Yarmouth, England and with her parents and two older brothers moved to Plymouth in Devon when she was 18 months old. Years later she returned to her birth place, a necessity due to her husband's employment.

Elizabeth is a mother of five, has 10 grandchildren and one great grandchild. Now retired she continues to keep busy through her children and grandchildren and is very dedicated to her faith.

Elizabeth has a great love for children and has found great joy and fulfilment in her roles as a mother and grandmother.

She decided to write this book to enable her to leave a record for her offspring and also as a possible help to those who find themselves in similar situations with their spouses, offspring or friends.

Contact Elizabeth:

www.elizabethcolley.co.uk/home.html
elizabeth@elizabethcolley.co.uk

* * *

I found myself caught up in the life of Elizabeth as she tells her story in a way which is personal yet embracing. Each time she encounters a challenge she seems to come through with faith, determination and inner courage which is both enlightening and instructive.

A good read and one I will pick up again and again if only to find encouragement when times are tough.

Michael Fielding-Smith